WHAT YOU ARE GETTING WRONG ABOUT
APPALACHIA

WHAT YOU ARE GETTING WRONG ABOUT
APPALACHIA

Elizabeth Catte

Belt Publishing

First edition 2018

ISBN: 978-0-9989041-4-6

Belt Publishing
1667 E. 40th Street #1G1
Cleveland, Ohio 44120
www.beltpublishing.com

Book design by Meredith Pangrace
Cover by David Wilson

INTRODUCTION

Six months before the 2016 presidential election, my partner and I moved from Tennessee to Texas, to a modest-size city best known for housing the largest oil refinery in the United States. It also has the distinction of having some of the highest rates of brain cancer, leukemia, stomach cancer, nervous system and skin disorders, and respiratory ailments in the country.

To convince ourselves that the move hadn't been a mistake, we talked often of our lives in Appalachia, where we lived in the shadow of paper mills, mines, and coal-burning plants. These discussions later became the justification for our sudden departure. We expected culture shock and homesickness in Texas, but we did not anticipate a baptism by sulfur dioxide, hexane, and pentane. If two people raised on heavy metals and slurry call time, it's fair to say that things might be fucked. By the time you read this, we'll be back home.

We longed for home for less clinical reasons as well. In Texas, upon hearing where we were from, everyone wanted to talk to us about a new book called *Hillbilly Elegy*, by a guy named J.D. Vance. The best-selling "memoir of a family and of a culture in crisis," now set to be turned into a film by Ron Howard, had become our political moment's favorite text for understanding the lives of disaffected Trump voters and had set "hillbillies" apart as a unique specimen of white woe. Using the template of his harrowing childhood, Vance remakes Appalachia in his own image as a place of alarming social decline, smoldering and misplaced resentment, and poor life choices. For Vance, Appalachia's only salvation is complete moral re-alignment coupled with the recognition that we should prioritize the economic investments of our social betters once more within the region.

It's a strange experience to be grilled about the social decline of "your people" less than five hundred yards from a refinery that gives poor African Americans cancer, but that is what happened to us. At the local university, people whose wall art had been eaten by pollution were suddenly and deeply fascinated by the tragedies of Appalachia.

"Why don't more people just leave?" they asked, while we silently calculated how much money we'd lose by moving back home. If we were destined to be poisoned by corporations and deprived of civil liberties by corrupt politicians, better the devil we knew, we reasoned.

Election season cast Appalachia as a uniquely tragic and toxic region. The press attempted to analyze what it presented as the extraordinary and singular pathologies of Appalachians, scolding audiences to get out of their bubbles and embrace empathy with the "forgotten America" before its residents elected Donald Trump. After the election, when it became too late, the pendulum swung in the opposite direction and empathy became heretical. Appalachia, political commenters proclaimed, could reap what it had sown.

There's not a single social problem in Appalachia, however, that can't be found elsewhere in our country. If you're looking for racism, religious fundamentalism, homophobia, addiction, unchecked capitalism, poverty, misogyny, and environmental destruction, we can deliver in spades. What a world it would be if Appalachians could contain that hate and ruin for the rest of the nation. But we can't.

In the region, we often speak of Appalachia as a mirror that reflects something troubling but recognizable back to the nation. Some cultures avoid mirrors in periods of mourning, afraid that the void created by grief might become a portal that causes something sinister to leak out. These days, an image like this seems fraught with extra meaning.

My partner and I went about our daily lives in Texas trying to convince people that the oil industry and the coal industry weren't fundamentally different to the person with undrinkable water. Cataloguing contemporary essays and interviews about the "Appalachia problem" became something of a hobby for me. I quickly discovered that the most telling aspect of these essays and interviews wasn't what they said about Appalachia, but what they didn't say.

According to the bulk of coverage about the region in the wake of Trump's election and the success of *Hillbilly Elegy*, currently at fifty weeks on the *New York Times* Best Seller list, I do not exist. My partner does not exist. Our families do not exist. Other individuals who do not exist include all nonwhite people, anyone with progressive politics, those who care about the environment, LGBTQ individuals, young folks, and a host of others who resemble the type of people you'll meet in this volume. The intentional omission of these voices fits a long tradition of casting Appalachia as a monolithic "other America."

While many regional groups experience this treatment, as scholar Elizabeth Engelhardt recently wrote in the journal *Southern Cultures*, "Appalachia stands out, however, in the sheer length of time that people have believed it could be explained simply, pithily, and concisely…again and again Appalachia is relegated to the past tense: 'out of time' and out of step with any contemporary present, much less a progressive future."

With this in mind, *What You Are Getting Wrong About Appalachia* has two objectives: to provide critical commentary about who benefits from the omission of these voices, using Appalachian history to push back against monolithic representations of the region, and to openly celebrate the lives, actions, and legacies of those ignored in popular commentary about Appalachia. The critic bell hooks wrote, "With critical awareness, we must recognize the spaces of openness and solidarity forged in the concrete experience of living in communities that were always present in radical spaces in Appalachia both then and now...I believe it is essential for unity and diversity to gather those seeds of progressive change and struggle that have long characterized the lives of some individuals."

I am a historian and *What You Are Getting Wrong About Appalachia* is filled with history, but it is not a comprehensive primer. Rather, it approaches history as the seeds that hooks describes, and hopes to plant in your mind something that might blossom if you examine the region more closely. This isn't, however, another one of those "voice for the voiceless" projects. For those who already know and celebrate a different Appalachia—and they are many—this is solidarity.

WHAT IS APPALACHIA?

Appalachia is, often simultaneously, a political construction, a vast geographic region, and a spot that occupies an unparalleled place in our cultural imagination. We'll start with the most basic information to get our bearings straight. Appalachia is an approximately 700,000-square-mile region of the eastern United States. It is loosely defined by the arc of the Appalachian Mountains that begins in Alabama and ends in New York, although the mountains continue into Canada.

There are thirteen states with Appalachian counties— Alabama, Mississippi, Georgia, South Carolina, North Carolina, Tennessee, Virginia, Kentucky, West Virginia, Ohio, Maryland, Pennsylvania, and New York—and West Virginia is the only state entirely within Appalachia. Appalachia's population is approximately twenty-five million individuals, although the rate of out-migration, especially among young adults, is high. You might think our biggest export is coal but it's actually people.

Defining Appalachian culture is often a top-down process, in which individuals with power or capital tell us who or what we are. These definitions tend to reduce people to pathologies, but can also include more clinical assessments, such as those that followed the creation of the Appalachian Regional Commission (ARC) in 1965. The ARC defined Appalachia as a coherent political entity during the Johnson administration's War on Poverty. It still exists (if precariously, at the moment) to monitor and create economic development within the region.

Although it made use of the existing geographical and cultural boundaries of the region, the ARC's primary lens was economic. One of its first tasks was to grade each county thought to be Appalachian on a scale of economic distress in order to administer federal aid efficiently. By its design, the region came to be defined by poverty, and subsequently poverty came to be defined by the region. This logic, like the War on Poverty itself, left an indelible imprint. You'll see what I mean soon.

The ARC's definition of Appalachia includes 420 counties, and therefore provides us with the most official scope of the region. There are, however, places like the Shenandoah Valley that are part of historic but not modern Appalachia. The reason? The area's political leaders simply didn't want to be part of the ARC's Appalachia and therefore severed themselves from the regional identity. Appalachia is nothing if not messily defined.

It is important to understand that whatever "Appalachian" is, it should first be seen as a flexible regional identity that has nothing to do with ethnicity. More than 80 percent of Appalachia's population identifies as white, but for the past thirty years, African American and Hispanic individuals have fueled more than half of Appalachia's population growth. Nonwhite Appalachians, as a group, tend to be younger and less likely to depopulate the region than their white counterparts. I'm hesitant to tell you *who* Appalachia is, but I can tell you who helps keep it alive: young individuals who work in racially diverse fields, including education, hospitality, and healthcare.

By several metrics, many parts of Appalachia are not places of robust racial and ethnic diversity, but the region is more diverse than it's presented in books, essays, and photographic projects. Only two Appalachian states—Kentucky and West Virginia— were identified among the ten "whitest" parts of the United States, behind Maine, Vermont, New Hampshire, Iowa, Idaho, and Wyoming.

Many Appalachians are working-class but their realities complicate definitions of the white working class that are incredibly popular at the moment. Coal miners, centered in political rhetoric as the face of the forgotten white working class, earn an average salary of $60,000 to $90,000 a year. It is more accurate to describe coal mining as a blue-collar profession that commands a middle-class salary, a rarity in our present moment and certainly an employment sector that is shrinking beyond hope. There are currently around 36,000 miners in the entire region. The *real* forgotten working-class citizens of Appalachia, much like the rest of the nation, are home health workers and Dollar General employees. They're more likely to be women, and their exemption from the stability offered by middle-class employment is not a recent phenomenon.

This volume will offer many thoughts about why we love these imaginary Appalachias, but it's important to first understand that the impulse to create them is old. One of my favorite historical documents is an editorial printed by a leftist newspaper serving southwestern Virginia coal country in the 1920s. The editorial mocked the national perception that Appalachia was home to a homogenous group of white people awaiting the attention and salvation of experts. Editor Bruce Crawford eviscerated a reporter who had traveled to the region to find "the mountain white," a "distinct race measuring up to all specifications" desired by "wild-eye reformers."

"In this little city buried away among the wretched ten thousand people over whom good-hearted philanthropists are currently weeping there was discovered a mountain white principal of a Norfolk high school and a high school teacher from Richmond," Crawford wrote, "and thereupon our traveler fled. He was last seen heading for the Kentucky mountains where we hope he will find people just as white and just as mountainous."

If you substitute "philanthropist" with "venture capitalist," you'll find that this reality has not shifted much for some.

Using Appalachians to fill made-to-order constituencies, anchored by race, is a tired game. Social upheaval, from the Civil War to the civil rights movement, often triggered, and still does, a larger fascination with Appalachia. These projections do a disservice to both Appalachians and other economically and socially disadvantaged groups by pitting their concerns against one another instead of connecting them.

Discussions of Appalachia's economy often trade on the perception that the region's people are dependent on government assistance, what we in the region sometimes call transfer payments. Historian Jessica Wilkerson recently wrote, "Writers and their readers play into political arguments that simplify Appalachia as a region that absorbs large amounts of government aid but gives back little, making it easier to condemn the people who live there."

Dependency narratives fuel popular talking points among individuals on both sides of the political aisle. They are often presented without acknowledgment that corporate welfare runs Appalachia. Corporate welfare allows business to shirk their tax burdens, hoard land, and wield enormous political influence while local communities suffer. Narratives of dependency conceal the uneven distribution of wealth that haunts Appalachia and indeed, much of the nation.

In 1979, Harvard University paid just $2.82 in annual property taxes on 11,182 acres of land in Martin County, Kentucky, an arrangement that received scrutiny after the ARC published an extensive study of land ownership in 1982. Appalachians are in the process of updating the land study, but what its original authors discovered in the 1980s is likely still true. Private businesses and out-of-state landowners do not carry anything close to an equitable local tax burden, making it impossible for communities to survive, let alone thrive.

Conservative political commenter Bill Kristol, for example, who often shames the poor via dependency narratives, earned his PhD from Harvard in 1979, during a time when impoverished Kentuckians subsidized his alma mater's endowment. These are connections that are as worthy of study as lurid assessments of Appalachian welfare rolls, but they are largely uninteresting to those often speaking for or about the region.

Many Appalachians are poor, but their poverty has a deep and coherent history rooted in economic exploitation. The coal industry is no longer a significant employment sector in Appalachia, but the dominance of coal's extractive logic has permanently ruined people and land in ways with which we must still contend. The people of Appalachia are predominately white, but the region is adding African American and Hispanic individuals at a rate faster than most of the nation. The average Appalachian is not, then, a white, hypermasculine coal miner facing the inevitable loss of economic strength and social status, but the average Appalachian's worldview may be impacted by individuals with cultural capital who are constantly assuming we are all made in that image.

If I sound cagey about providing resolute and emphatic markers of "Appalachia-ness," it is because people woefully overuse the term "Appalachian culture." This is particularly true in our current moment that fetishizes the presumed homogeneity and cohesiveness of the region and uses these characteristics to explain complex political and social realities. Appalachian scholars and activists often prefer to stress our interconnectedness to other regions and peoples rather than set ourselves apart as exceptions. Individuals in Appalachia, for example, offered support and solidarity to communities in Flint and Standing Rock, understanding that the struggle for clean water is local, but also national and global.

Many of the people you'll meet in this volume self-identify as Appalachian. I will not ascribe a culture to them, cohesive or otherwise, but I will locate them in shared experiences such as the struggle to arrest environmental destruction, to secure workers' rights, to demand clean water, and to preserve folkways. These struggles are ubiquitous in Appalachia but are not unique to the region. The individuals you'll encounter include Florence Reece, who fought mine wars with songs. Ollie Combs, a widow who put her body in the path of machines is here, and so is the Highlander Folk School, where civil rights leaders trained in nonviolent resistance. You'll get to know the people and projects of Appalshop and WMMT, media organizations focused on Appalachian issues, and individuals like Eula Hall, who tirelessly promoted rural health care.

Since Vance and his fans have made it acceptable to remake Appalachia in one's own image, let me do the same and create a volume with an image made in my own. Far from being monolithic, helpless, and degraded, this image of Appalachia is radical and diverse. This image of Appalachia does not deflect the problems of the region but simply recognizes the voices and actions of those who have struggled against them, often sacrificing their health, comfort, and even their lives. It is an image projected by bodies against machines and bodies on picket lines and bodies that most assuredly are not always white. This image of Appalachia won't be coming to a theater near you courtesy of Ron Howard, and we are all better for it.

PART I
APPALACHIA AND THE MAKING OF TRUMP COUNTRY

FROZEN IN TIME

On a frosty January morning in 2006, an explosion occurred in a coal mine owned by the International Coal Group in Sago, West Virginia. The explosion instantly killed one miner. Twelve others became trapped by debris, flames, and toxic gas. Their first shift after an extended New Year break had gone terribly wrong. All the missing men were fathers, some to young families, and the world watched as rescue crews tried to pinpoint their location in vain for two days.

Much of the news coverage focused on the anguish of the miners' families and how their grief reverberated in small communities like Sago or nearby Tallmansville. The families kept vigil at the Sago Baptist Church, just yards away from the mine, and national and international media crews kept watch with them. Sentimental and intimate narratives of faith and resilience overtook attention to the International Coal Group's notorious record of safety violations and fines.

Forty-eight hours after the explosion, an official working with rescue crews at the mine called the church to deliver news both heartbreaking and miraculous: the body of the one dead miner had provided an important clue in the discovery of the twelve living ones. The official informed families that rescue efforts were underway and activity at the mine intensified as celebrations at Sago Baptist Church became breaking news on every major network. "Their hope dimmed, but they never gave up," said ABC reporter Sonya Crawford, live from West Virginia.

Some families believed that rescue workers might triage the rescued men in the church and so they reorganized their surroundings as best they could for such a fraught reunion. They prepared and celebrated for three hours until a new report informed them that all miners save one had perished. A reporter for National Public Radio later confirmed that for most of that period, mine officials were aware there had been a grave miscommunication.

Captured on video, the celebrations of the families were frozen in time, and in their rebroadcast became a symbol of cruelty of the highest magnitude: false hope. Unfolding news coverage foregrounded the spectacle of decent but damaged people hoping in vain for a miracle. This made the reporting about the International Coal Group's lethal labor practices feel distant by comparison. As sociologist Rebecca Scott wrote of the incident, "Why miners might be afraid to report safety violations at a nonunion mine took second place to a story of a tight-knit, deeply religious community tortured on national television by the dramatic plot twist."

The coal company was indeed villanized by the press for its part in the tragedy, but not for its longstanding record of shirking state and federal safety regulations. The media presented families expressing anger toward the International Coal Group. But that anger was framed as a melodramatic response triggered by grief, not as a series of reactions compelled by the often abusive tension between mine operators and the communities that served as their workforce.

The media coverage of the Sago Mine disaster naturalized many practices in Appalachia that are not natural. It is not natural for individuals to mine coal, although it is a dominant industry in Appalachia and therefore a logical choice of employment. It is not natural for employees to die in the name of corporate profit and it is not natural to recycle the raw grief of devastated families into a spiritual lesson about sacrifice, as reporters did. Journalists sought details from families about dead miners' favorite scripture passages and analyzed them for clues that might indicate an acceptance of impeding death. It was as if the miners had undergone a meaningful spiritual trial instead of suffocating in the dark with their noses stuck in lunch pails because the rescue breathers supplied by the mine were useless.

When mine safety crews located letters written by the miners just before their deaths, reporters fixated on the last words of Martin Toler, Jr.: "It wasn't bad, I just went to sleep." A community and a nation seeking any sign of redemption from this tragedy naturalized even this most unnatural of deaths. Other, more invisible signs of redemption happened out of the public eye. Industry watchdogs challenged, in vain as it would happen, regulatory oversight of the coal industry and wrongful death lawsuits wound slowly through the courts.

During the 2016 presidential campaign, Appalachians were once again framed as decent but damaged people looking for a miracle. Donald Trump's campaign rhetoric centered the projection of a fantasy to "make America great again" by promising to correct the social and economic decline of disadvantaged white workers such as those who once populated the Sago Mine. "My guys," he often remarked, referring to miners, "don't get enough thanks."

Many Appalachians also engaged in fantasies of their own. The mayor of Buckhannon, West Virginia, just miles from the Sago Mine, told the *Washington Post* that Trump is "going to undo the damage to the coal industry and bring back the jobs, and all of our kids down there in North Carolina are going to come home." Every prestige publication from the *New Yorker* to *Vanity Fair* flocked to the region to capture a glimpse of the people whom they assumed stood ready to gamble the nation's political health on a last-ditch effort at self-preservation and, ultimately, false hope.

Following Trump's victory, pundits often engaged in a projection of a different fantasy, one where Appalachia might be isolated and left to reap what it had sown. For liberal political commentators there were no wealthy donors, white suburban evangelicals, or insular Floridian retirees responsible for Trump's victory, only hillbillies. This time, however, there would be no dignity in death. A month into his presidency, Trump appointed Wilbur Ross, the former owner of the Sago Mine, as his secretary of commerce. Some pundits and commenters applauded the decision for its awful symmetry.

For many Americans, the election simply cast "the Appalachian" in a role he appeared born to play: the harried and forgotten white everyman, using the only agency left in his bones to bring ruin on his countrymen and selfishly move our nation backward, not forward. Instead of serving as the instrument of his own torture, his false hope was now weaponized and aimed at the nation.

This projection of Appalachia is melodramatic and strategic in equal measure. It reflects a longstanding pattern of presenting Appalachia as a monolithic "other America" that defies narratives of progress. These narratives, however, are designed to allow you to applaud the casting choice without wondering who wrote the script. We'll watch the film here, but we're also going to stay for the credits.

APPALACHIA AND THE 2016 PRESIDENTAL ELECTION

Of the 2016 presidential election, *New York Times* international affairs correspondent Roger Cohen wrote, "The race is tightening once again because Trump's perceived character—a strong leader with a simple message, never flinching from a fight, cutting through political correctness with a bracing bluntness—resonates in places like Appalachia where courage, country, and cussedness are core values."

Cohen's dispatch is one of many that came to form a distinct genre of election writing: the "Trump Country" piece, which seeks to illuminate the values of Trump supporters using Appalachia—and most often West Virginia—as a model. "To understand Donald Trump's success," the composite argument flows, "you must understand

Appalachia." The march of the "Trump Country" genre became especially striking during a fraught election cycle marked by otherwise erratic coverage and scandal on both sides of the political aisle.

Sandwiched between email servers and *Access Hollywood* outtakes, Appalachians stood ready to offer human interest stories that demystified, or so the press assumed, the appeal of a distinct type of political annihilation. Pundits explained our socioeconomic realities to one another under the guise of educating a presumed audience of coastal elites whom, they argued, had become hardened to the plight of the forgotten American.

It is possible to glean, through the cumulative veneer of political analyses, think pieces, and grim photographs, some truth about the issues that vex Appalachia. But of equal importance is how this coverage reveals what vexes the nation about Appalachia. The voices of Appalachians as experts on their own condition are largely absent in the standard "Trump Country" think piece.

The emotional politics of this genre cast Appalachians as a mournful and dysfunctional "other" who represent the darkest failures of the American Dream while seeking to prescribe how we—the presumed audience of indifferent elites—should feel about their collective fate. Whether readers find these protagonists sympathetic or self-sabotaging, "Trump Country" writing leaves its audience to assume that Appalachians have not earned the right to belong in the narrative of American progress and are content to doom others to the same exclusion.

I first encountered the "Trump Country" genre in a February 2016 *Vanity Fair* essay by John Saward. "I am in West Virginia to understand Donald Trump," Saward explains in "Welcome to Trump Country, USA." Saward's offering is something of a travel dispatch of his accumulated experiences in Morgantown, Clarksburg, and Charleston. It begins with a tableau of Saward fondling a gun in a small-town strip club and ends with homespun mountain wisdom from a drifter. This structure implies that reality lies somewhere in between the maniacal Trump-supporting strip club denizens and the cosmically indifferent drifter. It also suggests that we should prepare for an age of extremes using Appalachia as a preview of coming attractions.

Saward takes pains to emphasize his difference from the subjects of his essay. What sets West Virginians most apart, according to him, is their longing and nostalgia for ordinary things. "You have never heard people speak so fondly, so intimately about hot dogs," he writes. "I have never cared as much about anything as this man did about a hot dog recommendation." When a local provides Saward with a list of restaurants to visit, he shares that "this will keep happening to me, people talking about the decency of other West Virginians and ordinary-seeming food like a dream."

This dream-walking offers sharp contrast to the realities Saward describes where "everywhere things are leaning, teetering; you might consider this metaphorically, but it is literally true, the houses are breaking." To collapse this sense of ruined nostalgia into a single anecdote, Saward lists half a dozen crumbling enterprises—car washes, bakeries, auto body shops—named after ordinary people, a "human with a name who had an idea for a place to do a thing and did it." In "Trump Country, USA," a car wash closed for the season isn't just a car wash, but a harbinger of a future when we might all wish for ordinary things in vain.

Early political forecasting compelled Saward and others to visit West Virginia in order to find "Trump Country." In December 2015, the polling firm Civis Analytics provided the *New York Times* with data suggesting Donald Trump would perform well in Appalachia and particularly West Virginia, his "best state" according to the *Times*. A national survey of 11,000 Republican-leaning voters indicated that Trump's strongest supporters tended to be individuals who once registered Democrat but presently vote Republican, a phenomenon that isn't uncommon in the South and Appalachia as a holdover from union-influenced politics.

Nate Cohn, who analyzed the data for the *Times*, argued that candidate Trump was the best fit among individuals "on the periphery of the G.O.P. coalition." The Civis data also suggested, however, that eight out of the ten best congressional districts for Trump were in New York, and particularly on Long Island. Other news sites often highlighted the metrics of Trump's appeal in West Virginia in early 2016 as well. A *FiveThirtyEight* report, for example, suggested that many of Trump's Facebook "likes" came from users in West Virginia.

Examining election predictions in the first days of the Trump administration is like looking at one's reflection in a dirty mirror. Many polls and forecasts show something recognizable amongst other distortions, and this phenomenon is also true of the "Trump Country" genre, which built momentum as primary season approached and all but exploded after the West Virginia Republican primary in May 2016. It's important to acknowledge that Donald Trump *did* (and still does) enjoy strong support amongst many Appalachians and West Virginians. And these supporters often framed their justification by identifying their alienation from both parties, triggered by unmet political expectations and white racial anxiety. None of their positions, however, were unique to Appalachia or West Virginia.

What we know now, of course, is that these narratives employed a sleight of hand that used working-class people to illustrate the priorities and voting preferences of white middle-class and affluent individuals. The *Washington Post* and other outlets issued correctives, reporting that "the narrative that attributes Trump's victory to a 'coalition of mostly blue-collar and white working-class voters' just doesn't square with election data."

To be fair, the Trump campaign, and the continued rhetoric used by his administration, participated heavily in this myth making. Individuals on both sides of the political aisle, however, are reluctant to change the narrative. Months after the election, hastily written diagnostic texts about the white working class, such as Joan

Williams's *White Working Class: Overcoming Class Cluelessness in America,* were published, creating further entrenchment.

No place demonstrates the uneasy reality of the "Trump Country" genre better than McDowell County, which sits firmly in West Virginia's historic coal fields and once had the largest population of African American individuals in the state. In our present climate, however, McDowell County is a majority-white community that shares the worst local employment and health outcomes with neighboring coal counties Mingo and Logan.

During the 2016 presidential campaign, McDowell County became synonymous with "Trump Country." It was the subject of profiles for the *Guardian, Huffington Post, Circa,* the *National Post, CNN,* and *CBS,* with mention in dozens more about West Virginia or Appalachia at large. A widely-shared video segment in the *Guardian* in October 2016 asserted that "Donald Trump was more popular in McDowell County than anywhere else in America."

Coverage of past elections told a different story about McDowell County and West Virginia. In 2008, McDowell County was among the few counties in West Virginia where Democrats held on to a margin of victory. A more modest number of reporters and journalists dove into the history of the county and its politics to explain that phenomenon. The documentary *Divide,* for example, explores the 2008 election through the eyes of union organizer Sebert Pertee, who canvassed for Barack Obama in coal country. In those days, West Virginia was "Hillary Country," with Clinton beating Obama in the state's Democratic primary by substantial margins, including in McDowell County, where she won more than 70 percent of the vote.

Obama won McDowell County by 8 percent in the 2008 general election, but lost West Virginia. By 2012, West Virginia was entirely red. West Virginia Democrats appeared so disillusioned with their party that they gave Keith Russell Judd, a federal corrections inmate in Texas, 40 percent of their vote in the 2012 Democratic primary.

It isn't difficult to locate compelling political angles in West Virginia's coal country, which was solidly Democratic for forty years. Analysts point to the dwindling strength of unions and the coal industry's hostility to environmental regulations as the chief political frustrations turning the tide. Both Republican and Democratic state politicians have pushed "war on coal" narratives that suggest industry decline is the product of overregulation, not market forces and competition from cheaper energy. With often little difference among their elected leaders, West Virginians have witnessed a remarkable political indifference to economic diversification.

Economic strategies most often prioritized financial and tax incentives that helped larger corporations and staved off losses to coal company profits. These strategies offered a united message from Republicans and Democrats that the way forward requires the free flow of capital in the hands of businesses, not people. It's a position that pits workers against the environment in the battle for economic stability. It also accepts that the replacement of permanent and benefitted jobs with unstable low-wage employment is a natural by-product of corporate growth.

Political candidates committed to labor and environmental issues don't often fare well in West Virginia, not because they're unpopular with the electorate but because pro-business moderates from both parties invest in their failure. Take the case of Charlotte Pritt, who in 1996 defeated current Senator Joe Manchin in the gubernatorial primary with an anti-corporate-interest platform. Instead of endorsing Pritt, members of the Democratic Party's elite, including Manchin himself, touted a "Democrats for Underwood" coalition, supporting the Republican nominee. Pritt narrowly lost the election.

Following a hiatus, Pritt has returned to politics, announcing in 2016 her intention to once again run for governor, this time affiliated with West Virginia's Mountain Party. Pritt isn't the only candidate inspired by Bernie Sanders's success in the region. Joe

Manchin's opposition to populists like Pritt helped elevate him to the rank of senator, but he'll soon face off against Bernie Sanders acolyte and political newcomer Paula Swearengin, a single mother from Coal City, West Virginia. As she told the *New Republic*'s Sarah Jones, "It's time for us to fight back."

In the interview, Swearengin recalls a moment at a town hall meeting in Charleston when Joe Manchin tried to incite the crowd against her by framing her call for cleaner, safer jobs as hostile to working men and women. Interjecting layers of such divisiveness is typical of the establishment's political playbook for both parties in Appalachia, and particularly West Virginia. To be pro-environment and pro-worker is to walk a tightrope where individuals on either end hope you fall. In March 2016, Hillary Clinton did just that.

Two months before the West Virginia primary, Clinton made remarks at a CNN-sponsored town hall that would continue to haunt her campaign in West Virginia and Appalachia. Asked what her platform could offer struggling poor and working-class white voters, Clinton used coal country as an example of a region that would benefit from the creation of new economic opportunities under a development plan that utilized clean energy technology to fuel job growth.

"I'm the only candidate which has a policy about how to bring economic growth using clean renewable energy as the key into coal country," she said, "Because we're going to put a lot of coal miners and coal companies out of business, right?" She continued, "And we're going to make it clear that we don't want to forget those people. Those people labored in those mines for generations, losing their health, often losing their lives to turn on our lights and power our factories."

A move away from fossil fuels, including coal, was not, Clinton insisted, a "move away from the people who did the best they could to produce the energy that we relied on." But these remarks played badly in coal country. The Trump campaign handily transformed her comment about out-of-business coal workers into a threat.

It's not possible for anyone with more than passing knowledge of Appalachia and the coal industry to listen to those comments without cringing, regardless of one's political affiliation. Clinton's remarks about out-of-work miners are a ghastly but honest flub. But her tone—"those people who did the best they could"—and her poor appropriation of the "coal keeps the lights on" slogan are equally problematic. "Coal keeps the lights on" is often the rallying cry of those condemning the "war on coal," but I suspect even the most progressive among us have been tempted to lob the phrase at someone clueless about the human cost of their energy. People didn't "do their best" to keep the nation's lights on; they died.

Analysts often pointed to Clinton's remarks as the moment she sealed her fate in West Virginia and Appalachia. A somewhat excruciating campaign stop in Williamson, West Virginia, just before the state's May primary seemed to confirm this prediction. During a roundtable session, an unemployed former coal miner named Bo Copley grilled Clinton about her town hall remarks, resulting in a lukewarm apology from the candidate. After clarifying her earlier statements, Clinton told Copley, "I do feel a little bit sad and sorry that I gave folks the reason, or the excuse, to be so upset with me...I'm here because I want you to know whether people vote for me or not, whether they yell at me or not, is not going to affect what I'm going to try to do to help."

His confrontation with Clinton made Copley into a coal country celebrity, and he later told *Fox News* host Neil Cavuto that he did not feel particularly nervous during the meeting because he "speaks for a lot of people in our area." Copley also appeared on ABC, CBS, and Yahoo News, personalizing the "war on coal" narrative by sharing his own struggle to find stable employment after his former employer Arch Coal filed for bankruptcy. Clinton lost the

West Virginia Democratic primary later that month. Bernie Sanders cleared more than 50 percent of the vote, winning every county. Donald Trump received more than 70 percent of the vote in the state's Republican primary, also winning every county in the state.

The "Trump Country" genre exploded after the West Virginia primary. Both Trump and Sanders won parts of Appalachia by large margins. The media made a broad and unconvincing attempt to de-legitimize Sanders's popularity in Appalachia. This attempt wasn't forcefully challenged when Sanders ceased to be a viable presidential candidate, but it has returned with a vengeance among the left. Alex Seitz-Wald from MSNBC, for example, found Trump's victory in parts of Appalachia to be "weird" and suggested that "mischievous Trump supporters sought to damage Clinton, the likely Democratic nominee, by voting for Sanders."

Many networks picked up an exit poll that suggested as many as one-third of West Virginian Sanders voters would choose Trump over Clinton in the November election. Projection of this sort was somewhat unique to West Virginia. All primary results bear the mark of "delegate math"—predictions for the remaining primary elections and how these votes might yield clues for the general election—but analysts gave the West Virginia primary more intense scrutiny. The outsized attention of this and other coverage was often at odds with the fact the state only commands five Electoral College votes and is not particularly instrumental in presidential elections.

The media often declared, as Canada's *National Post* did in the early fall of 2016 that "there are few better places to understand how Donald Trump could become the U.S. president than McDowell County." CNN called McDowell county residents "members of a forgotten tribe," pointing to Trump's share of the primary that yielded the candidate 90 percent of the Republican vote. But that figure amounted to just over 700 votes in actual numbers split between a pool of candidates narrowed by the primary's timing.

CNN's segment also featured another minor celebrity of the election cycle, a ninety-three-year-old gas station owner named Ed Shepard who appeared in a number of articles and essays distilling wisdom about coal country's decline. Shepard became the living personification of this decline, often photographed in his cluttered gas station that appeared only to serve the press. His presence in "Trump Country" pieces was so ubiquitous that when a post-election segment by West Virginia Public Radio implored listeners to reach out to Trump voters, it included "dusty gas station" owners in its roll call.

McDowell County and other coal country counties also became the subject of a glossy *New Yorker* profile in October 2016. "In the Heart of Trump Country," written by Larissa MacFarquhar, featured intimate interviews with West Virginia voters alongside bespoke images taken by Magnum photographer Alec Soth. Of one Trump voter, MacFarquhar writes, "He is not the Appalachian Trump supporter as many people elsewhere imagine him—ignorant, racist, appalled by the idea of a female President or a black President, suspicious and frightened of immigrants and Muslims, with a threatened job or no job at all, addicted to OxyContin."

It's revealing that MacFarquhar imagines her piece both within and outside the "Trump Country" genre. While noting its power to reduce voters to a series of caricatures and stereotypes, she nevertheless uses its momentum to tell what she presumes to be a more nuanced story using the same individuals to decode the rise of Trump to her audience. "Everywhere you go in West Virginia, there are wrecks of houses half-destroyed by fire or fallen in with age," the text notes, under a photograph of a perfectly intact house with a only pair of children's tricycles visible in its surroundings.

Her piece ends with a scene of an enthusiastic Trump supporter caring for neglected graves in local cemeteries including, we learn, a slave cemetery. This finale blithely implies that many Trump voters might not be the enemies of equality we've imagined them to be, but rather individuals trapped in limbo, stuck in communities of the barely living and the dead.

The media also used other Appalachian communities to explain Trump's popularity. Roger Cohen filed a dispatch from eastern Kentucky for the *New York Times* in September 2016 that emphasized how Trump's character resonated in down-and-out coal country. "For anyone used to New York chatter, or for that matter London or Paris chatter, Kentucky is a through-the-looking-glass experience," he writes. But in Lewis Carroll's books, curious creatures exist in a world without time or direction, and things break that cannot be repaired.

For Cohen, what makes eastern Kentucky—a nine-hour drive from New York City—Wonderland isn't its unfamiliar-to-him surroundings, but the issues that preoccupy many of the individuals he interviews. Many are, Cohen observes, "blue lives matter" supporters. Most are incensed by wage stagnation. But according to Cohen, these attitudes are different than those found in New York, where a white police officer strangled an African American man to death for selling cigarettes, or Paris, France, where police and citizens joined forces to destroy the temporary housing of Muslim migrants.

"Somewhere on the winding road from whites-only bathrooms to choose-your-gender bathrooms, many white, blue-collar Kentucky workers—and the state is 85.1% white—feel their country got lost," he concludes. The voices of eastern Kentucky's African American residents—whose numbers equal around 10 percent of the population of Paris—are absent from Cohen's dispatch.

Momentum to visit and re-visit Appalachia to decode the ascendency of Trump also sustained itself through the publication of *Hillbilly Elegy*, and Vance's consequent media ubiquity as chief analyzer of the white working class. The proliferation of Vance interviews featured in articles with titles such as "How hillbillies helped Trump shake politics" and "Trump: Tribune of poor white people" did little to complicate what had become an entrenched belief that Appalachia, and to a lesser extent the Rust Belt, was ground zero for Trumpism.

The website *Daily Kos* even began running predictions that treated Appalachia as one very large state, offering a graphic-heavy analysis of Trump's domination in the region. Analysis and prediction of this sort, which the site continued to use even after the election, implied that Appalachia would be singularly responsible for a Trump victory.

Appalachia's vote most assuredly helped Trump's victory, but so did votes in Alaska, Arkansas, Florida, Idaho, Indiana, Iowa, Kansas, Louisiana, Michigan, Mississippi, Missouri, Nebraska, North Dakota, Ohio, Oklahoma, South Carolina, South Dakota, Texas, Utah, Wisconsin, and Wyoming. Trump also fared well in some congressional districts in blue states such as California and New York. Eastern Long Island and Staten Island voted for Trump by substantial margins. As pundits scrambled to determine what went so amiss in exit polling, the nation awoke on November 9 to the news that we were all now residents of Trump Country.

Pew Research reported that Trump, with his largest wins among white individuals without college degrees, fared well among all white voters. Trump's popularity among white women received a great deal of press attention and often became the portal to broader discussions of race. Jesse Washington wrote that "one sentiment rang loudest in many African-American hearts and minds: the election shows where we really stand. Now the truth is plain to see, many said—the truth about how an uncomfortable percentage of white people view the concerns and lives of their black fellow citizens."

Many African American writers were not surprised that so many white individuals stood ready to uphold a racialized status quo. Sociologist Tressie McMillan Cottom wrote in the *Atlantic* that "Those of us who know our whites know one thing above all else: whiteness defends itself." Others pushed back at this narrative, seeking more nuance in election statistics. Kelly Dittmar from the Center for American Women and Politics at Rutgers, commented, "I think this narrative about Clinton failing to win white women really overshadows the strong support she had among all women, and women of color in particular." This optimistic interpretation of election results was not uncommon in postelection bloodletting. Many white individuals were aghast to see their progressive credentials questioned by proxy. Pundits previously content to cast an entire region as universally white and poor now demanded the absolution of nuance for themselves.

Generously used human interest stories from Appalachia freshened up older discourse. Producing, consuming, and commenting on stories about down-and-out white voters became a specific form of political engagement. As one commenter wrote on the *Guardian*'s videologue of McDowell County, "It is unhelpful, as this piece makes clear, to demonize or belittle those who voted for Trump out of desperation. Rather, we need to hear their desperation and help them."

Trump's inauguration, however, brought a new set of emotional politics to bear on the "Trump Country" genre, particularly among progressive individuals. Unrewarded by calls for empathy for the Trump voter, pundits pivoted as Trump's brutal executive orders called for immigration bans, deportations, threats to healthcare, and the dismantling of environmental protections. Markos Moulitsas of *Daily Kos*, for example, proclaimed that Americans should "be happy for coal miners losing their health insurance." From *New York Magazine* to the *New Republic*, many progressive outlets ran pieces that expressed a performative wish, quite simply, for the deaths of millions of people.

It is possible to observe in the "Trump Country" genre a conversation between pre-and-post election commentaries. To interpret this conversation generously, one might suggest that the authors aren't angry with Appalachia at large, but instead are striking back at what the seemingly endless array of pre-election "Trump Country" pieces told them to think or feel. Many are fed up that reasonable discussions of racism among Trump's base keep getting deflected with copies of *Hillbilly Elegy.* Most writers appear exhausted by relentless election re-litigation that suggests #Berniewouldhavewon by citing his popularity in red states.

What these pieces lack, however, is an acknowledgment that this dynamic fits a longstanding pattern of "expert" analysis of Appalachia. Appalachians are the subjects of the "Trump Country" genre, not its creators. Indeed, the primary factor determining expertise in this and other eras is social and geographic distance from Appalachia.

"Trump Country" pieces share a willingness to use flawed representations of Appalachia to shore up narratives of an extreme "other America" that can be condemned or redeemed to suit one's purpose. This is the region's most conventional narrative, popularized for more than 150 years by individuals who enhanced their own prestige or economic fortunes by presenting Appalachia as a space filled with contradictions that only intelligent outside observers could see and act on.

Prolific Appalachian historian Ronald Eller wrote, "We *know* Appalachia exists because we need it to define what we are not. It is the 'other America' because the very idea of Appalachia convinces us of the righteousness of our own lives." Appalachia is real, but it exists in our cultural imagination as a mythical place where uncomfortable truths become projected and compartmentalized.

INVENTING THE APPALACHIAN "OTHER"

To understand how Appalachians came to be defined as "the other" requires a trip back in time, but the strategies employed will be recognizable to modern eyes. People in power use and recycle these strategies not because it's enjoyable to read lurid tales of a pathological "other"—although that certainly informs part of the allure—but because they are profitable. And if you trace a flawed narrative about Appalachia back far enough, you'll often find someone making a profit.

What follows is the briefest slice of Appalachian history, from the Civil War to the Great Depression, to emphasize how the invention of the "other" went hand in hand with the desire to broker a rich land from poor people. This process unfolded with intent and malice, often to justify the most exploitative manifestations of capitalism in order to make them appear natural or necessary.

The belief that Appalachians represented a legibly distinct culture—what historian Henry Shapiro called a "strange and peculiar people"—formed just after the Civil War. Ways of life that existed in Appalachia before the Civil War were shaped by the forced migration of indigenous peoples and the resulting encroachment of white European settlement, along with mercantile networks carved out by distant land speculators.

After the war, speculators and industrialists became more strategic in their acquisition of land. Appalachia's timberlands and mineral regions created eager competition among investors. Advances in rail transportation, in turn, facilitated more efficient movement of people and cargo to and from the region. Charles Dudley Warner, a travel writer and co-author with Mark Twain of *The Gilded Age*, wrote in 1888 of his travels in Kentucky, "I saw enough to comprehend why eager purchasers are buying forests and mining rights, why great companies, American or English, are planting themselves there and laying the foundations of cities, why gigantic railway corporations are straining every nerve to penetrate the mineral and forest hearts of the region." He concluded, "It is a race for the prize."

That prize, of course, was the accumulation of personal wealth in the name of modernization and progress. Although Appalachia's first extractive industries also included copper and mica, coal quickly became the region's most valuable resource, fueling much of the nation's industrial expansion, from the rebuilding of railroads to the generation of power. Mineral agents purchased enormous tracts of land while at the same time sending scouts into coal-rich areas of the region to offer individual landowners quick cash for their subterranean mineral rights.

Coal companies often justified their expansion and the recruitment of local populations into their workforce as benevolent actions that would bring backward mountaineers into their own as equal participants in America's expanding spirit of industry. Outsiders consumed the circumstances of "mountain life" in the form of travel writing or "local color" essays. Horace Kephart, a writer who lived among Appalachians in Tennessee during the 1910s, wrote that "in Far Appalachia, it seemed I might realize the past in the present, seeing with my own eyes what life must have been to my pioneer ancestors." This projection also suited the needs of industrialists who benefited from narratives that suggested the people of the region should be "developed" and put to purpose.

The idea of Appalachia as a peculiar and untamed corner of America grew in popularity during the early twentieth century. This shared belief facilitated a number of experiments and outcomes within the region. Outside entrepreneurs pushed the limits of industry in the name of modernization, folklorists sought and collected "primitive" arts, missionaries brought religion to the "unchurched," and industrialists drew from a vast pool of expendable labor.

According to Shapiro, these outcomes and their justifications formed a "secondary vision of Appalachia as an area in need of assistance from outside agencies." Experts, he continued, "insisted vigorously on the vision of Appalachian 'otherness'…and their discussions on the nature and meaning of Appalachian otherness were rarely made with reference to the real conditions of mountain life or the normal complexity of social and economic conditions which prevailed in the mountains as in every other section of the nation."

Narratives of Appalachian "otherness" often worked too well. America at the turn of the twentieth century had little patience for upstarts who complicated notions of progress and national unity. Just as immigrants and African Americans in the Northeast faced hostility for diluting the social and cultural norms of elites, Appalachians were also regarded with an assimilationist gaze. Since the dilemmas of "otherness" were so often self-created and abstract—the real conditions of life in Appalachia or in immigrant neighborhoods did not reflect what elites envisioned them to be—they could not be solved. Appalachians were not uncivilized in the way that intellectuals imagined them to be, and the symptoms of their "backwardness"—favoring different religious practices, for example—did not constitute pressing social issues.

In order to reconcile these irreconcilable Americas, Appalachian "otherness" became a form of deviance. As Shapiro observed, outsiders "defined Appalachia as a discrete region and the mountaineers as a distinct people, and responded to abstract dilemmas which this 'fact' seemed to pose without asking whether it was a 'true' fact, or indeed whether it was *still* a true fact in 1920 as it might have been in 1900 or 1870."

For industrialists, the national perception of Appalachia as a blighted and unnatural place aided their economic expansion. The most degraded of all Appalachians were those who, by chance or intent, had not taken their rightful place in the region's mines and mills. One community located near the Tug River along the West Virginia-Kentucky border came to be synonymous with deviance of the highest order. During a period of rapid industrial expansion, the "primitive" ways of the Tug River Valley ceased to be innocent or quaint and instead became sinister and lethal.

MURDERLAND

Not far from my home is Pigeon Forge, Tennessee, a place where visitors can dig into "feudin' fried chicken" at the Hatfield-McCoy Dinner Show, a glitzy comedic musical featuring down-home Southern fixins. The Hatfield-McCoy feud remains one of the most legendary moments in Appalachian history. This nineteenth-century epic family rivalry between the West Virginian Hatfields and the Kentuckian McCoys has served as the basis for films, cartoons, musicals, documentaries, historical fiction, and reality television shows. There's even a reference to the feud in the online role-playing game *World of Warcraft*. A cottage industry of Hatfield-McCoy tourism is popular in Appalachia and one needs not travel to Kentucky or West Virginia to consume the Hatfield-McCoy spectacle. Much like fixins at the Hatfield-McCoy Dinner Show, this cultural fare is all-you-can-eat.

Popular interpretations of the feud emphasize idiosyncratic and primitive aspects of mountain culture: log cabins, bonnets and overalls, impenetrable accents, moonshine, fiddles, and banjos. The tourism industry presents the Hatfields and McCoys, and their various analogues, as patriarchal, lawless, prone to violence, uncivilized, stubborn, barely educated or articulate, highly isolated, and alarmingly impoverished. Even Vance claims, by way of explaining his family dynamics, that he is a descendent. "If you're familiar with the famous Hatfield-McCoy family feud back in the 1860s, '70s, and '80s in the United States, my family was an integral part of that," he writes.

In our present day, the Hatfield-McCoy feud feels folksy and humorous. We indulge in the mildest of subversive impulses by enjoying exaggerated but harmless representations of anarchy and lawlessness. But make no mistake, the feud was a real event that occurred in Appalachia at the turn of the twentieth century. Today, however, it is also a story that reflects a number of abstract dilemmas imposed on the region and demonstrates just how consumable lurid stories of Appalachian folkways can be. To spoil the plot somewhat, the Hatfield-McCoy feud is more than just a legendary example of bad blood. It is also a tale of what happened when coarse representations of an untamed "other" boomeranged back to the region.

In the most basic interpretation of the conflict, two families separated by Tug Fork of the Big Sandy River carried home Civil War-era rivalries that spiraled into a feud that lasted for the better part of twelve years. Shortly after the war ended, a former Union soldier on the McCoy side was murdered, presumably at the hands of former Confederate soldiers on the Hatfield side. Thus the feud began, with periods of dormancy interrupted by livestock theft, murder, and unwise and doomed romances between younger members of the Hatfield and McCoy families.

Local law enforcement grew tired of the families' tit-for-tat and took to the mountains to round up what they described as a community at war. Law enforcement captured members of both families, and in 1889, the court secured the conviction of several members of the Hatfield family for murders connected to an 1888 massacre. National newspapers and curious journalists followed the feud, some traveling to the region in the hope of meeting depraved and lawless mountaineers engaging in old fashioned frontier justice. Patriarch "Devil" Anse Hatfield appeared often in menacing sketches and photographs posing with rifles, and by many accounts enjoyed his celebrity. Local developers, politicians, and business people, however, did not.

The feud provided sensational material for individuals preaching the gospel of Appalachian "otherness." In the late-1880s, New York reporter T.C. Crawford traveled to Appalachia—which he called "Murderland"—to obtain material for a book about the feud published in 1889 as *An American Vendetta: A Story of Barbarism in the United States*. According to Crawford, "barbaric mountaineers" populated Appalachia, a place where a primitive race of people lived in "a blood-stained wilderness" that was "as remote as Central Africa."

Crawford's dispatches inspired a number of fictional accounts of blood-feuds in Appalachia, including Harvard writer John Fox, Jr.'s *A Cumberland Vendetta* in 1895. Fox describes his feuding protagonist as "a dreamy-looking little fellow, and one may easily find his like throughout the Cumberland—paler than his fellows from staying indoors, with half-haunted face, and eyes that are deeply pathetic when not cunning…he suffered to do his pleasure—nothing, or much that is strange without comment."

Academics also offered their analysis of Appalachia's primitive culture by dissecting the Hatfield-McCoy spectacle. In 1901 the University of Chicago's S.S. MacClintock chronicled the feud in the *American Journal of Sociology*. After noting that "blood-revenges" are nonexistent in civilized society, MacClintock writes, "The proportion of murder to other crimes in the mountains is strikingly large. Stealing is rare, killing is common." In MacClintock's learned opinion, the causes of the feud are attributable to primitive kinship societies in Appalachia, the sensitivities of mountaineers, and their sheer idleness. "There are so few industries and responsibilities of any kind that even a feud is a relief from the awful monotony," he argues. He was just one in a cohort of sad academics who wrote paper after paper trying to unlock the secrets of the universe by revealing that rural people sometimes steal livestock and hate their neighbors.

We can't leave out locals from this group of profiteers as well. As historian Altina L. Waller notes, local businessmen and politicians benefitted from the idea that modern employment and industry were just what the region needed to clean up its act. Through their efforts to bring state "justice" to the Tug River Valley—to make the region seem more hospitable to outside developers—up-and-comers often exacerbated tensions, even during periods when the families were at peace. Today, Appalachians are free to profit off the feud through tourism, but only if we present it through the most clichéd of regional hillbilly stereotypes.

Intellectuals like MacClintock looked to other solutions when the triumph of law and order in the valley proved to be short-lived. One popular solution was simply capitalism. If Appalachians could be tamed and put to industrial purpose, these theories suggested, then they might be spared the bloodshed, vice, and moral degeneracy natural to their primitive existence. This was music to the ears of developers, who justified economic expansion by contending that modern employment would bring order and harmony to the mountains and save mountaineers from their own worst impulses in the process.

WHEN I GET TO HELL, I WILL GET THE COAL AND PILE IT UP ON THEM

A desire to "tame" Appalachians for the benefit of industry often lurked behind twentieth-century theories of Appalachian "otherness." Although industrialists deployed region-specific narratives to justify the development of Appalachia, widely held attitudes about the social position of the poor aided them in this. Late nineteenth and early twentieth-century Social Darwinism, for example, posited that wealth and privilege fell naturally to those who most deserved them and that social differences between the rich and the poor reflected differences in their innate abilities.

The poor might improve their station through hard work and industry, but those of greater means owed them nothing in this struggle. This theory befit a world enthralled by the free market and the competitive accumulation of capital. Many industrialists felt little responsibility to their workforce, often believing that their social assistance would encourage an undesirable overpopulation of the lower classes.

By contrast, some industrialists were paternalistic in their attitudes toward the working poor who labored in their factories, mines, and mills. Industrialists demanded obedience from their workers, much like children, and in return showed their benevolence in the form of housing, entertainment, or more comfortable working conditions. What these two social attitudes shared was the belief that power and capital came naturally to those of greater ability and that safe working conditions and other residual benefits of labor were a sign of their generosity, not the obligations of a good and moral business.

In Appalachia, narratives that presented mountaineers as helpless and otherwise doomed without industrial purpose abounded. Coal barons credited their industry with bringing order and harmony to an uncivilized place, but what actually came to the mountains was a vast system of economic exploitation, facilitated through violence and malice by both outside developers and compliant local elites. The company town became emblematic of this new industrial order. Miners and other coal workers in West Virginia, eastern Kentucky, and southwestern Virginia—Appalachia's historic coal fields—often lived in privately owned towns, which grew to outnumber independent and unincorporated communities.

In addition to recruiting local mountaineers, coal companies imported labor from other parts of the United States. African American miners were common in Appalachia at this time, 20 to 50 percent of the workforce. Recent European immigrants, particularly from Italy and Poland, also populated the coal fields. In coal camps and company towns, the nation's accumulated "others" worked and lived in a coercive environment designed, as one coal operator explained, "to have men concentrated so as to have proper supervision over them, to better control them in times of labor agitation and threatened strikes."

Proper supervision meant armed security, often drafted from private detective agencies and local law enforcement. As you might imagine, it proved difficult to convince workers to risk their lives daily in the dark holes of the earth for almost no money. Bribing local law enforcement and politicians to maintain coercive practices became part of the cost of doing business for coal companies. Political corruption flourished in the coal fields. In West Virginia, Logan County sheriff Don Chafin made $50,000 a year in his prime in kickbacks from the Logan County Coal Operators Association.

Coal companies exhibited a distinctly violent hysteria toward organized labor and suppressed union agitation by any means available. In 1912, for example, private detectives attempted to curtail a strike by repeatedly terrorizing the wives and children of miners in the Paint Creek-Cabin Creek area of West Virginia with machine gun fire. For many miners, however, unionization was a matter of life and death. One could die in the mines or march, and many chose to march. Mary "Mother" Jones, who cofounded the Industrial Workers of the World, said of West Virginia, "The story of coal is always the same. It is a dark story. For a second's more sunlight, men must fight like tigers. For the privilege of seeing the color of their children's eyes by the light of the sun, fathers must fight as beasts of the jungle."

Labor agitation in West Virginia is immortalized in many songs and union anthems. "Law in the West Virginia Hills," written around 1912, contains a verse that describes the experience of watching private detectives beat pregnant women to the point of miscarriage. "My sister saw these cruelties," the singer explains, "as they terrorized the town. She saw them murder unborn babies and kick these helpless women down." This is what martial law looked like in the coal fields, and it came often. Using nonunionized labor gave southern West Virginian coal companies a competitive market advantage over unionized mines and made their West Virginian coal fields frequent targets for efforts to expand the United Mine Workers of America. Each campaign brought bloodshed, but none loom larger than the uprisings of 1920 and 1921 that culminated in the Battle of Blair Mountain, the final chapter of West Virginia's mine wars.

I COME CREEPING

In 1920, a group of private detectives employed by the Baldwin-Felts Agency on behalf of the Stone Mountain Coal Company traveled to Matewan, West Virginia, to evict the families of miners from their company housing after they had attempted to join the union, a common union-busting tactic. Unlike their counterparts in the notoriously corrupt Logan County, the miners in Matewan, in Mingo County, had a number of important allies. One of these was Mingo County police chief Sid Hatfield, whom journalist Hamilton Nolan recently memorialized as "a strongly pro-union man who was also a bit of a psycho killer."

Hatfield, a legendary figure sometimes called the "Terror of the Tug," secured arrest warrants for the crew of Baldwin-Felts agents when they couldn't produce eviction notices, and he deputized a number of local miners to help him keep the peace. Not surprisingly, arming angry miners as a peacekeeping strategy did not work. Instead it led to a spectacular gunfight in downtown Matewan that killed Albert and Lee Felts, the villainous brothers who helped run the detective agency, along with five other private detectives. Hatfield's reputation became outsized, a mountain David in a world of Goliaths. While awaiting trial for the murder of Albert Felts, Hatfield shot a silent film for the United Mine Workers of America in which he played himself in a re-enactment of the gunfight.

Despite being acquitted on the murder charge, Hatfield ultimately proved to be vulnerable. In 1921, Thomas Felts, aiming to avenge his brothers' deaths, pressured McDowell County officials to indict Hatfield on charges stemming from a year-old incident.

When Hatfield appeared for the trial on August 1, Baldwin-Felts agents murdered him on the courthouse steps.

A hero was dead and tensions in the coal fields reached a fever pitch. The United Mine Workers had planned a demonstration, but organizers wondered if it was wise to sponsor industrial action in such a fraught environment. Mother Jones, it appears, had the privilege of the deciding vote. The United Mine Workers rallied at the capitol in Charleston, presenting a list of demands to the governor. A week later the governor refused all union demands and coal country went to war.

By the end of August, more than 13,000 individuals stood ready to take whatever form of justice most satisfied them from the West Virginian coal fields. For some, it was the liberation of miners from economic exploitation through union solidarity. For others, it was revenge: one of the most popular songs hummed in the assembled crowds was a bright little anthem about murdering Don Chafin, set to the tune of union hymn "Solidarity Forever."

It was the most significant labor uprising in United States history and the largest show of armed resistance in America since the Civil War. The assembled crowds included doctors, lawyers, women, farmers, children, business owners, and teachers. Their number included around 2,000 African American men and women, some who were born into slavery like George Echols who said, "I was raised a slave. My master and mistress called me and I answered, and I know the time when I was a slave, and I felt just like we feel now." Many assembled wore red bandanas around their neck, the only insignia available, leading their enemies to call them "rednecks." One miner wrote, "I call it a darn solid mass of different colors and tribes, blended together, woven, bound, interlocked, tongued and grooved and glued together in one body."

This is how I prefer to remember the Battle of Blair Mountain. There was, of course, a battle; a weeklong campaign during which miners fought valiantly against a private army that the National Rifle Association would later praise for "using every type of firearm produced in the United States." Its arsenal included not only firearms, but also gas explosives and aerial bombs deployed by private planes. But not even Mother Jones herself could call back the miners, who had to be driven off the mountain by federal troops. I have no claim of kinship to this story, but I imagine it often, the unafraid and justice-seeking united in one body snaking through the mountains to reclaim themselves. "How do you come to Mingo?" the miners' scouts asked, to identify their allies. "I come creeping," came the answer. Like vines they went, slow and purposeful and of the earth, fed at long-last on sunlight.

A HISTORY OF THE WHOLE PEOPLE

There are a number of different ways to evaluate the Battle of Blair Mountain and what it meant to West Virginia and Appalachia, organized labor, and the larger body of exploited workers in the United States. On a practical level, the battle and the violent suppression that followed weakened the United Mine Workers of America in West Virginia. One conventional historical narrative is that organized labor in West Virginia languished until Franklin Roosevelt's more labor-friendly administration set about creating pro-union legislation.

But there's another side to this story, one told through the hysterical reactions of the coal industry and its political allies at the mere mention of the Battle of Blair Mountain. By the 1930s, the coal industry had spent sixty years crafting the story of Appalachia as a region and of Appalachians primed for their benevolent development. When the people tried to reclaim their narrative and write their own history, all hell broke loose.

In 1935, the government proposed an ambitious plan to commission a history for every state, written by ordinary men and women. The idea behind what became the Federal Writers'

Project's American Guide Series was New Deal logic through and through. The project would put unemployed men and women to work, giving them relief from the Depression, and would use their labor to create something for the public good. In a time of dramatic social upheaval, many Americans—including those in the White House—felt an urgency to repurpose history to show the nation its populist roots. This, of course, was a political strategy that suited the Democrats' new vision for America, but it was also attuned to a deeper social need to explore a shared past during a moment when many were overcome with feelings of isolation.

The government envisioned the American Guide Series, as one Federal Writers' Project official observed, as a "history of the whole people…in which the people are historians as well as the history, telling their own stories in their own words—Everyman's history, for Everyman to read." In both theory and practice, the series raised uncomfortable questions about who constituted "the whole people" and what aspects of a "people's history" should be remembered. Federal and state officials censored the contributions of local authors heavily, actions that resulted in power struggles and political crises in Appalachia, particularly in West Virginia.

West Virginia's history of radical labor uprising proved to be a source of consternation for both Federal Writers' Project officials and state leaders. Left in the hands of local politicians, the West Virginia guidebook would have been a bland piece of coal industry public relations. As historian Jerry Thomas writes, "The leadership of both major political parties in West Virginia had long clung to the notion that organized labor, especially among miners, was a deadly conspiracy to be ignored publically and suppressed privately. Legitimizing labor by acknowledging its importance along with heroes of the frontier and the Civil War was a bitter pill for the established political community to swallow."

There are few historical events that I wish I could have witnessed firsthand, but on that short list is the moment that

Homer Holt, West Virginia's anti-union governor, learned that his state's history would be compiled by Bruce Crawford, the former editor of a left-wing union newspaper who was once shot while providing aid to striking miners and who called for a "producers' dictatorship" to overthrow the elite. Crawford took over the direction of the West Virginia Federal Writers' Project in 1938, after the first version of the state guide was nearly complete, and his conflicts with Holt became the stuff of local legend. (One of the great joys of writing this book was discovering that Bruce Crawford cut his teeth publishing a leftist newspaper in Norton, Virginia, where my people are from. It moves me that Crawford, however indirectly, fought for my family.)

Opponents of organized labor saw in Crawford's guidebook the potential to indulge "every tint and taint of radicalism." One Republican asked if the schoolhouses of West Virginia would be painted "not the red of the Red, White, and Blue…but the 'red' of the revolutionary?" Holt refused to authorize the publication of any guidebook written under Crawford, calling his re-written manuscript "propaganda from start to finish." In other words, the history of the people, in Holt's view, did not include the mine wars, labor agitation, or industrialists murdering Black workers with impunity through silicosis. Mother Jones never came to West Virginia, Blair Mountain never happened, and coal camps were as clean as a pin and populated only by whites.

Holt attempted to have Crawford dismissed and censured, and the manuscript languished until 1940, when Holt lost his re-election to his rival Matthew Neely. The federal government and its proxies at Oxford University Press published a mostly un-sanitized version of the book—*West Virginia: A Guide to the Mountain State*—in 1941 with the new governor's approval. It included a separate essay on organized labor in the state, as intended.

"The workmen's struggle in West Virginia for better working conditions and the right to organize has been a long one and, in the mining industry particularly, one marked by bitter conflict, violence, and tragic incident," it began with purpose that yes, in retrospect, was a bit radical. My favorite part of the chapter is not the text itself, but the somewhat out of place and whimsical sketch of an apple tree that concludes it. It reminds me of Helen Lewis, an elder Appalachian activist who wants to reclaim former mining land with apple orchards.

It's tempting to conclude this story with that sentimental image. Believe me, there are people in Appalachia reading this, thinking, "Oh Helen, you are too pure for this world," and I hate to wreck that with pettiness. But I will. As governor, Holt had established an agency called the State Publicity Committee, which became an instrument of the coal industry. Public relations propaganda about how positively wonderful the coal industry was flowed through the agency with the governor's seal of approval. But when Holt lost his reelection bid, the Publicity Committee got a new director. That man was Bruce Crawford.

WE ARE ALL RESIDENTS OF TRUMP COUNTRY

The battle to control the narratives of Appalachia went through many phases between the Civil War and the Great Depression, but we see a number of similar themes. Chief among them is the tendency of those in power to represent rank-and-file Appalachians as helpless and in need of intervention to earn their place in the story of American progress. In the period of rapid industrial expansion, this outlook facilitated the coercion of poor Appalachian workers into an exploitative system of labor and created powerful and prevalent narratives of Appalachian "otherness."

When the national narrative of progress shifted during the Great Depression to emphasize the contributions of the worker, the powerful reacted with hostility. They attempted to censor meaningful episodes of Appalachian history that suggested its people had more than earned their belonging and had, in fact, instigated positive social change in their own right. The "Trump Country" genre borrows the worst aspects of both impulses. The press often used the perceived helplessness of Appalachians to naturalize a specific political choice and ignored the voices and stories of those attempting to call a different outcome into being.

Before moving on to see how this battle played out in more recent history, let's check in with West Virginia's coal country one last time. Was McDowell County "Trump County" in the way that the media purported? Using gritty black and white photographs, the *Huffington Post* offered McDowell County as a "glimpse at the America that voted Trump into office." The use of the phrase "the America" to set Appalachia apart from the places inhabited by the article's presumed audience is telling; Appalachians, of course, don't need an invitation from flagship outlets to take a look at their surroundings. A CBS segment on McDowell County hosted by Ted Koppel concurred with the *Huffington Post*: "McDowell County was, unambiguously, Trump Country."

In the 2016 presidential election, McDowell County gave Donald Trump 4,614 votes and Hillary Clinton 1,429. The election rolls indicate that there are 17,508 registered voters in the county, although the actual number in circulation is likely lower. Nevertheless, Trump won McDowell County during an election that had a historically low voter turnout for the county. If we use reported numbers we find that only 27 percent of McDowell County voters supported Trump.

Bo Copley, a coal country celebrity after his tense encounter with Hillary Clinton, reported to CNN's Van Jones after the election that Clinton's position on the future of coal mining was irrelevant. He was never going to support a "pro-abortion" candidate because of his religious beliefs, a very common position among conservatives nationwide. And Ed Shepard, the elderly gas station attendant regarded as a source of regional wisdom by many outlets? He simply didn't vote. "I didn't vote in this election. I see no meaning of this. Whoever goes to the White House will do whatever he/she wants to do and won't give a damn about us," he told the *Huffington Post*.

If it is appropriate to label a small but visible subgroup as unambiguously representative of 25 million people inhabiting a geographic region spanning over 700,000 square miles, then we should ask a number of questions. Where were the "Bernie Country" pieces about Appalachia? There are more people in Appalachia who identify as African American than Scots-Irish, so where were the essays that dove into the complex negotiations of Appalachian-ness and blackness through the lens of the election? I associate contemporary eastern Kentucky with grassroots prison abolition, so where were the essays about how a presumed Trump victory would imperil that work? West Virginia has the highest concentration of transgender teenagers in the country, so why didn't anyone examine this facet of "Trump Country" and how the election might reverberate in their lives? In April, filmmakers in West Virginia hosted the fourth Appalachian Queer Film Festival. How did that play out at the close of Trump's first one hundred days in office?

Many things about Appalachia may be true simultaneously. The support for Trump may be real, too strong for my comfort, and it may also be true that there are many who hoped and still hope for a different outcome. It might be true that much of the region is overwhelmingly white, but it is also true that there are few towns or cities in Appalachia without a visible African American or Latino community. Constructions of the region as "all-white" to satisfy a particular fetish about the white working class maliciously erase individuals whose lives also matter.

To be sure, there are many stories about Trump and Appalachia that can and must be told, they're just not the ones that individuals with powerful platforms want to tell.

As Jessica Wilkerson observes, "Ignoring or erasing stories of community organizing and coalition building makes it easier to paint Appalachians as perpetual victims of economic decline or hypocrites who receive government aid without reciprocity."

How does life go on in "Trump Country" for those of us who never lived in "Trump Country" to begin with? It goes on much the same as it always did. For me, I will try to build power with likeminded individuals and challenge the institutions that harm us. I won't do that by reaching across political divides that are far more complicated here than you can image. I'll do it by exercising the basic principles of mutual aid and community defense. The people of Appalachia have never needed empathy; what we need is solidarity, real and true, which comes from understanding that the harm done to me is connected to the harm done to you.

bell hooks writes that "we will not change or convert folks without extending the forgiveness…that is essential for the building of communities of solidarity." I admit this election has caused setbacks for me on this path of grace. But in my world, it is not immaterial to me as someone who wishes to achieve specific outcomes that, for example, a "landslide" victory of 90 percent of the vote represents, in some places, fewer than one thousand people. It is not immaterial to me that many saw a different way forward. And it is not immaterial to me that individuals with power and capital still subject us, in our pain, to the sense of entitlement that allows even the most ambiguous of outcomes to be presented as a concise narrative, richly rewarding, satisfying to everyone but us.

Entitlement. It is, I think, the perfect word to bear in mind as the next chapter unfolds. Elegy is another. In a former life, I used to be a translator. It was, as it turns out, a completely useless profession, but it did allow me to spend several years reading poetry. While reading Greek poetry, my professors warned us to be careful of the double meaning of elegies; they were, it seems, often written as political propaganda.

PART II

HILLBILLY ELEGY AND THE RACIAL BAGGAGE OF J.D. VANCE'S "GREATER APPALACHIA"

A CAMERA IS A GUN

An hour before his murder, Canadian filmmaker Hugh O'Connor paid a young coal miner in Jeremiah, Kentucky, ten dollars for the use of his image in an exhibition film destined for the 1968 World's Fair. Covered in coal dust and cradling his child, the miner "had an expression of total despair," O'Connor's film crew remembered, "It was an extraordinary shot—so evocative of the despair of the region." The miner lived in a rented cottage among half a dozen other families set in a small clearing of land owned by Hobart Ison, who offered the cottages for ten dollars a month. For the price of a month's rent, the miner traded his image to a man whom his landlord would soon shoot and kill.

Ison, armed with a revolver, discovered O'Connor and his crew of five on his land just minutes after the filmmakers concluded their final shot. Ison ordered the men off his property but, weighed down by their equipment, the crew could not escape before Ison opened fire. He put one bullet in the camera, and a second in Hugh O'Connor's chest. According to O'Connor's producer, the filmmaker fell to his knees calling out to Ison, "Why did you have to do that?" before dying moments later.

The film company that hired O'Connor sent funds to Kentucky to help the commonwealth's attorney prosecute Ison, but its influence and wealth had little return in Letcher County. Even though Ison was known as an eccentric in Jeremiah, he enjoyed enormous community support after his arrest. "Streams of people came to visit Ison in jail before he was released on bail," Calvin Trillin wrote in the *New Yorker*. "Women from around Jeremiah baked him cakes." After an unsuccessful jury selection—no locals would even entertain the idea of Ison's guilt—a judge ordered the trial moved to nearby Harlan County. The first trial resulted in a hung jury, and Ison struck a deal, pleading guilty to involuntary manslaughter, midway through the second. He served one year in prison and died ten years later in 1978 at the age of eighty.

In 1999, Kentucky filmmaker Elizabeth Barret released *Stranger with a Camera*, a documentary exploring the context of the murder. In answering the film's central question—what brought these two men face-to-face on that day in 1967—Barret examines the impact of Appalachian "poverty pictures": images of lurid white poverty intended to shock middle-class audiences. Their creators often cited "poverty pictures" as a necessary catalyst for social change, exposing the alarming conditions of inequality in Appalachia. In reality, Barret argues, outsiders often "mined images in the way the companies mined the coal."

What becomes of people, Barret's documentary asks, when they become a wellspring for the nation's pity or disgust? One answer lies in Barret's interview with Mason Eldridge, the miner filmed by O'Connor just before his death. Eldridge is sincere, open, and friendly, but never lifts his eyes to Barret's camera.

One man lowered his eyes, another lifted his gun. Both responses, Barret suggests, are reactions to exploitation and shame. The visual archive of Appalachia created in the 1960s focused exclusively on the region's deprivation. In the process of its creation it provided the raw material for a new moral position about the lot of the poor. The belief that poverty is a character flaw—a demonstration of moral weakness—hangs over every image of a barefoot child or unemployed miner.

"The American dream has become a nightmare," the BBC announced in a 1967 documentary about eastern Kentucky. To be Appalachian was to be heir to a distinct kind of wretchedness, endlessly performed before an international audience. This created layers of shame in communities like Jeremiah. The more well-to-do often came to resent the poor for acting as the enticement for those with greedy cameras. "The ties that bind communities together are not always positive," Barret observes.

As the local with a camera, Barret has a connection to both Ison and O'Connor that is painful and real. Her interviews with O'Connor's family and colleagues are among the film's most wrenching scenes, precisely because they possess a clarity about O'Connor's death that Barret and her community will never—and perhaps *should* never—experience. All are sympathetic to the suffering caused by the willful misrepresentation of a community. They forgive. But for all the soul-searching performed by Barret, it is one of O'Connor's Canadian colleagues, Colin Low, who delivers the most electrifying lines in the documentary: "A camera is like a gun," he explains, "It's threatening. It's invasive; it is exploitative…and it's not always true."

I thought about *Stranger with a Camera* often last year, believing that the time had come to experience, as Barret did, what it's like to live among so many people who have snapped and have put their pain and resentment in the service of terrible outcomes. Their politics will kill good people. If a camera is a gun, then surely a vote can be too.

But I also thought about Barret's work for another reason. Outdated theories about a culture of poverty in Appalachia, honed in the 1960s, had become popular once more thanks to *Hillbilly Elegy*. Much like the visual archive generated during the War on Poverty, *Elegy* sells white middle-class observers an invasive and exploitative story of the region. For white people uncomfortable with images of the civil rights struggles and the realities of Black life those images depicted, an endless stream of sensationalized white poverty offered them an escape—a window into a more recognizable world of suffering. This intimacy, both now and then, does not equal less contempt, just more value for the viewer and creator.

In some cases the parallels stretch back further, to the exaggerated stories of mountain life created by local color writers during the Hatfield and McCoy era. Appalachian Studies scholar Jordan Laney recently described the experience of reading *Hillbilly Elegy* while preparing snippets of local color for her class. "How did journalists and correspondents for the *New York Times* as well as scholars not catch these acts of generalizing and aggrandizing on behalf of elite readers?" she asks. "How did we trade in the breadth of diversity the region has to offer for one view? While reading *Hillbilly Elegy* I thought, here is how. *This* is how places and people become caricatures of themselves, ourselves."

COMMODIFYING THE "OTHER"

Men who shirk employment and women who lack the appropriate amount of shame for their illegitimate children populate the world of *Elegy*. Instead of attending church, the people of *Elegy* worship material desires beyond their means and use welfare fraud in the service of their doomed pursuits. "This is the reality of our community," Vance writes. "It's about a naked druggie destroying what little of value that exists in her life…Our homes are a chaotic mess. We scream and yell at each other like we are spectators at a football game. At least one member of the family uses drugs—sometimes the father, sometimes the mother, sometimes both. At especially stressful times, we'll hit and punch each other, all in front of the rest of the family, including young children."

His use of the world "we" transforms the personal reality of his difficult childhood into a universal experience. The broadest point made by *Elegy* on the basis of this experience is that "public policy can help, but there is no government that can fix these problems for us.

These problems were not created by governments or corporations or anyone else. We created them, only we can fix them."

The argument that corporations did not help create the problems of Appalachia is stunningly ahistorical, but not even the most problematic claim Vance makes.

The *National Review*, which employed Vance as an occasional contributor, was positively gleeful about the book's release. Their review, one of the first, all but explicitly congratulated the author for at long last proving that white Appalachians have "followed the black underclass and Native Americans not just into family disintegration, addiction, and other pathologies, but also perhaps into the most important self-sabotage of all, the crippling delusion that they cannot improve their lot by their own effort." The *American Conservative* also helped sustain the first wave of publicity for the book in the summer of 2016, and took particular relish in republishing comments from liberal-leaning and nonwhite individuals in praise of it.

"Would you believe," columnist Rod Dreher excitedly shared, "that two other liberal correspondents who wrote to praise Vance are black and gay—one of them is an immigrant—and both identified Vance's discussion about moral agency among the poor as critically important?" For many conservatives, the beauty of *Elegy* was not just what it said about the lot of poor white Americans, but what it implied about Black Americans as well. Conservatives believed that *Elegy* would make their intellectual platforming about the moral failures of the poor colorblind in a way that would retroactively vindicate them for viciously deploying the same stereotypes against nonwhite people for decades.

It is not possible, in my view, to separate *Elegy* from the public persona crafted by Vance over the course of his book tour, his numerous engagements as a political pundit, and his still-forming plans to revitalize the region through venture capitalism and a possible run for political office. The most interesting trait conveyed by this persona is its overperformed humility.

Despite graduating from Yale, authoring a best-selling book about the region, and commanding what he calls a "preposterous amount of money" for public speaking engagements, Vance consistently denies claims that he is acting as an "expert" about Appalachia and, to a lesser extent, the Rust Belt. He is simply an individual burdened with the dual identity of both cosmopolitan elite and hillbilly everyman, performing what he calls his "civic responsibility" to contribute his talent and energy to solving social problems.

"It's an indictment of our media culture that a group that includes tens of millions of people is effectively represented by one guy. I feel sort of uncomfortable being the guy," he told the *Washington Post*. He bemoans this trend as he appears on major news networks analyzing the region's white working class, and as he delivers TED talks about Appalachia. He is so uncomfortable being the spokesperson for a region whose personal experiences have become symbolic of the realities of millions that he recently sold the film rights to *Elegy* to Ron Howard.

Perhaps Vance *is* an incredibly rare breed of humble venture capitalist turned regional memoirist turned social reformer. But perhaps it is wise to consider if this humility is just a strategy. By framing his celebrity as "reluctant," Vance shores up an image of his insight as accidentally and authentically profound and not, for example, shaped by his three years writing for a conservative publication, or his mentorship under controversial figures like Amy Chua, author of *Battle Hymn of the Tiger Mother*, and the entrepreneur and political activist Peter Thiel.

Of course, Vance makes no secret of his conservative leanings, but he displays a remarkable tendency to opt himself in and out of the genealogy of conservative writers on race and poverty as it suits his purpose. Using pseudo-academic theories of "brain drain"—including citations—he justified the belief shared in a *New York Times* op-ed that venture capitalism might stimulate the region. But when he was pressed on social media about the negative implications of his framework, Vance stated, "I don't infer that [the region] suffers from brain drain. My point was simply to discuss the attraction of home." The "accidental profundity" granted to Vance must be gratifying, if not something of a backwards compliment, but it also allows him to escape more explicit associations with other controversial work and theories.

In early 2017, the conservative intellectual and white supremacist Charles Murray embarked on a campus speaking tour funded by the American Enterprise Institute, where he is a senior fellow. University communities protested Murray's presence on their campus forcefully, leading to a particularly tense incident at Middlebury College in Vermont. Murray's lectures refreshed observations he shared in his now five-year-old book, *Coming Apart: The State of White America, 1960-2010*, though he adapted them to our current political moment. Many protesters, however, were alarmed by the scientific racism standing at the center of his career as a public intellectual.

Best known for co-authoring 1994's *The Bell Curve: Intelligence and Class Structure in American Life*, Murray made his name peddling what the *New York Times* called "racial pornography." His belief that African Americans are genetically predisposed to lower intelligence, manifested through IQ testing, became part of the lexicon of the culture of poverty through his suggestion that many forms of government assistance harmed society by encouraging the overpopulation of the intellectually undesirable. "For women near the poverty line in most countries in the contemporary West, a baby is either free or profitable, depending on the specific terms of the welfare system in her country," he wrote.

Murray, like many other conservative social scientists, enjoys playing an old game in which he occasionally flips his script to contempt for poor white individuals in order to mitigate the racist origins and applications of his beliefs. *Coming Apart*, for example, proved to be less controversial than *The Bell Curve*, although he frequently uses the success of the former to re-affirm the latter. He recently told author and podcaster Sam Harris that he not only stands by *The Bell Curve*'s conclusion, he feels that his evidence is stronger and more relevant than ever.

Disruptions of Murray's invited talks at Middlebury and elsewhere ignited a widespread debate about free speech and the twenty-first-century university. Some pragmatic observers of this debate suggested a telling workaround to mitigate campus controversy. Columnist Louis Shucker, for example, wrote in the *Reading Eagle* that "Perhaps a better selection would have been J.D. Vance, author of the best-selling *Hillbilly Elegy*." The implication is that while the two share similar beliefs about poverty and race, Vance is baggage-free in a way that Murray is not.

Let us give him some baggage, then.

A RACIAL PRISM

Vance uses an enduring myth about race in Appalachia and parts of the Rust Belt to give *Hillbilly Elegy* its organizational logic. It is, in essence, the magic that transforms *Elegy* from a memoir of a person to the memoir of a culture. Central to *Elegy* is Vance's belief that both historic and modern white Appalachian people share a common ethnic ancestry in the form of Scots-Irish heritage. He connects this belief, in turn, to his claim that shared ethnic heritage has endowed contemporary white Appalachians with certain innate characteristics that hold the key to understanding why their home is, as he puts it, a "hub of misery."

The shared culture of Appalachia, he writes, is one that "increasingly encourages social decay instead of counteracting it." It's worth noting that my distinction—"white Appalachians"—is not one that Vance uses. In the world of *Elegy*, all Appalachians are white.

He writes in the introduction, "The Scots-Irish are one of the most distinctive subgroups in America. As one observer noted, 'In traveling across America, the Scots-Irish have consistently blown my mind as far and away the most persistent and unchanging regional subculture in the country. The family structures, religion and politics, and social lives all remain unchanged compared to the wholesale abandonment of tradition that's occurred nearly everywhere else.'"

This observation, presented as an endorsement of Vance's construction of Scots-Irish whiteness, comes from a blog post written for *Discover* magazine in 2012 entitled "The Scots-Irish as Indigenous People," by a writer named Razib Khan. It argues that bracketing all white people together in discussions of white privilege leads to "perverse situations." As an example, the post offers the hypothetical case of Malia Obama, who would be able to "benefit from affirmative action" due to her race, while the "child of a poor family from Appalachia who was white would not gain any preference."

Vance continues, "This distinctive embrace of cultural tradition comes along with many good traits—an intense sense of loyalty, a fierce dedication to family and country—but also many bad ones. We do not like outsiders or people who are different from us, whether the difference lies in how they look, how they act, or most important, how they talk." This shared Scots-Irish ancestry and the traits that it endows, Vance argues, means that "the culture of Greater Appalachia is remarkably cohesive." This cohesion, in turn, has caused white Appalachians to reproduce, almost literally, negative social outcomes in isolation.

"We pass that isolation down to our children," he writes, invoking visions of genetic heredity. He points out that "many of us have dropped out of the labor force or have chosen not to relocate for better opportunities. Our men suffer from a peculiar crisis of masculinity in which some of the traits that our culture inculcates make it difficult to succeed in a changing world." He concludes his introduction with the hope that readers might gain from his memoir an appreciation for "how class and family affect the poor without filtering their views through a racial prism." This is a remarkable statement, because the only way to truly understand *Hillbilly Elegy* is through a racial prism, one that centers a mythical form of whiteness that has a dangerous history.

In his willingness to present white Appalachians as a distinct ethnic entity, Vance has placed himself in a disturbing lineage of intellectuals who relished what they presumed to be the malleable whiteness of Appalachia for its ability to either prove or disprove cultural beliefs about race. This belief manifests in two ways. The first, which we've already begun to unpack, is the more modern and recognizable conservative impulse to discount the links between structural racism and inequality. Why can't poor Black people get ahead? It's not racism or the structural inequality caused by racism, many conservatives argue, because then what would explain the realities of poor white people?

The lives of poor white people, especially those with the additional burdens of addiction or legal issues, become the empirical proof for conservatives that we have based our attention to racism on fractured logic. The irony, of course, is that even as we become the ambassadors of this colorblind worldview, poor white people can't escape the generic moralizing of their betters, who got a head start honing their brand of arrogant tough love and hard truths on Black communities.

The second manifestation of this belief is more complicated and requires us to go back in time to discover how white Appalachians were transformed, in some intellectual circles, as a race or "stock" unto their own and the consequences that followed. Vance didn't invent this particular fiction, he simply exploits it to provide his narrative with a cohesiveness and cultural weight that wouldn't otherwise exist. Why does that matter? There's a phenomenon that occurs in Appalachia in which writers and other creatives who anchor their work in ideas about the unique genetic or cultural qualities of Appalachians also harbor close associations with eugenicists. Yes, *eugenicists*.

It turns out that if you create and sell a version of Appalachia as a place filled with defective people, eugenicists start paying attention to your work. The esteem, as you'll learn, isn't unilateral. I'm going to give you three examples—and no prizes for guessing that the mutual appreciation between Vance and Charles Murray is among them—but each episode is separated by enough time and space to demonstrate that this is both a pattern that persists and a pattern that should be stopped.

THE SCOTS-IRISH MYTH IN POPULAR HISTORY

What's up with the culture of Appalachia? The first thing we should pull apart is that there's really no such thing as "Greater Appalachia," a term Vance likes to use. Maintaining flexible definitions of Appalachia is appropriate. The boundaries of the region reflect tensions between political, cultural, and geographic definitions. But the use of the term "Greater Appalachia" in *Elegy* is telling. Like so much of *Elegy*, "Greater Appalachia" is the invention of a particular political moment that has been recycled to serve a different political moment. "Greater Appalachia" is connected to a 2012 work of popular history by Colin Woodard called *American Nations*. Woodard, by way of explaining contemporary political divisions and particularly the rise of the Tea Party, posits that America is not one nation, but eleven.

Each nation, according to Woodard, possesses a "dominant culture" that holds clues for understanding positions on everything from gun control to racial equality. One such nation is "Greater Appalachia." Woodard writes, "Founded in the eighteenth century by wave upon wave of settlers from the war-ravaged borderlands of Northern Ireland, northern England, and the Scottish lowlands… it transplanted a culture formed in a state of near constant danger and upheaval, characterized by a warrior ethic and commitment to personal sovereignty and individual liberty."

Elegy invokes other popular histories as well, particularly Virginian politician Jim Webb's 2004 book *Born Fighting: How the Scots-Irish Shaped America*. Although Webb is a Democrat, he shares with Vance a history of military service. Webb uses this tradition as a starting point for his exploration of Scots-Irish culture. *Born Fighting* is largely a recuperation and celebration of Webb's Scots-Irish "redneck" roots, which he credits for his successes in military and political leadership. Like Vance, Webb maintains that the people of Appalachia have unique genetic qualifications that have produced innate traits and characteristics. Webb, however, is more laudatory of these than Vance and even goes so far as to state that "no other group has been more denigrated, attacked, and even feared by America's evermore connected ruling elites" than the Scots-Irish.

Webb's work relies on shaky historical foundations but exploits a very real turn in scholarship, primarily among a segment of Civil War historians, which sought to explain class differences among white people in a slave-holding society. Starting in the 1980s, Civil War historians Grady McWhiney and Forrest McDonald pioneered the "Celtic thesis," which argued on the basis of remedial research that more than half of white Southerners, prior to the Civil War, were of Celtic stock. Because of this, the thesis suggests, the Civil War might be best understood not as a rejection of slavery, but as a clash of white ethnicities as Anglo-Saxon elites in the North attempted to forcibly impose their worldview on a largely Celtic South.

If you think that tangentially plugging into academic scholarship exonerates Vance, I have bad news. McWhiney and McDonald, with their emphasis on shared white ethnic heritage and their mitigation of white supremacy as a feature of antebellum life, became the favorite historians of white nationalist groups. McWhiney even participated in the founding of his own hate-group, the League of the South, which recently came to Pikeville,

Kentucky, to rally with Nazis in defense of white families. Both McWhiney and McDonald eventually denounced the League of the South, but not before helping to legitimize a particularly virulent strain of neo-Confederate thought still in currency.

Writer John Thomason observes in the *New Inquiry* that, "Even as Vance wags his finger at the vices of his fellow hillbillies, he cannot help but to insist on the innocence of their whiteness." In constructing the Scots-Irish—the hillbillies in *Hillbilly Elegy*— as a race unto their own, Vance can argue that it's simply their innate characteristics that have set them on this destructive path that culminated in the election of Donald Trump, not their racism. This is highly alarming and, as Thomason argues, makes racial determinism "more palpable to audiences that might normally be on guard against white nationalism."

Vance appears to take particular relish in using inaccurate constructions of Appalachian whiteness to complicate universal notions of white privilege. As he told Ezra Klein from *Vox*, "The problem, as I see it, is that we haven't necessarily developed a great vocabulary to describe disadvantage in a newer, much more culturally diverse country…it's not just that talking to that kid [a young person from West Virginia] about white privilege is not an especially useful way to understand his real disadvantage. It's that it actually makes it harder for him to see the disadvantages that other people face." The idea that confronting racism risks irrevocably alienating individuals of all races is both a common and predictable strain of thought among conservatives, but it becomes more sinister when it is propped up by the belief that the white individuals in question represent a disadvantaged race unto themselves.

In *Elegy* and in Vance's comments about *Elegy*'s subjects, white Appalachians take on the qualities of an oppressed minority much in the same way that conservative individuals view African Americans: as people who have suffered hardships but ultimately are only holding themselves back. This construction allows conservative intellectuals to talk around stale stereotypes of African Americans and other nonwhite individuals while holding up the exaggerated degradations of a white group thought to defy evidence of white privilege.

Vance drags the Obama family into discussions and sets them against poor white Appalachians. In his interview with Ezra Klein, he noted, "One of the points I tried to make is that if you're asking the son of a West Virginia coal miner to check his privilege or to appreciate ways that, say, Barack Obama's daughters are going to be privileged or underprivileged relative in certain ways, I think you're asking too much from basic cognition," echoing the blog post comments he cites in *Elegy*. It is telling how infrequently individuals who are both Black and Appalachian appear in his remarks. While bemoaning our basic cognition, he takes liberties with his own by refusing to acknowledge that not all West Virginians or coal miners are white.

Is it true that white Appalachians share a common Scots-Irish heritage and does this heritage inform our social position in the modern world? The answer to both questions is an emphatic "no." Apart from myths and legends, there is no basis for the belief that historic or contemporary white Appalachians share a distinct culture informed by their homogenous ethnic heritage. In fact, fighting that myth has been the life's work of many Appalachian historians.

The myth that Vance draws upon, borrowed from *American Nations*, *Born Fighting,* and other popular histories, often goes something like this. Once upon a time, during some indeterminate period usually in the eighteenth century, white people who weren't pilgrims came to America. Those of Irish or Scottish origins were attracted to the eastern mountains because mountains were in their blood or some other romantic nonsense. These groups settled there and became the Scots-Irish.

The mountains, in turn, provided powerful insulation against the forces of the modern world and allowed the Scots-Irish to retain "old world" characteristics such as a clannish or tribal family structure, peculiar forms of speech, and the general traits of an "honor" or "warrior" culture that included a propensity for violence and feuding. Over time, this shared heritage became the presumed basis for certain ethnocultural deficiencies due to over- and interbreeding.

The work of modern Appalachian historian Wilma Dunaway provides a sharp corrective to the myth, which she calls the "ethnic homogeneity thesis." Her scholarly work is filled with insight, drawn from primary sources of the Appalachian frontier and archaeological evidence, that eighteenth-century Appalachia was a fusion of a variety of European ethnic groups and other groups that reflected African and indigenous descent.

Archaeologists also address this myth in their work. Audrey Horning writes in her work on migration, "The southern upland region attracted settlers not only from the British borderlands… but from all over North American colonial regions as well as from France, the Palatinate and West Africa, while later drawing from eastern and southern Europe."

Scots-Irish heritage is real, but the exaggerated dominance of its influence in the region is often put into the service of a variety of outcomes. In the early twentieth century, reformers utilized the belief that Appalachians were of "pioneer stock" in the application of a new social order that sought to curb the influence of "undesirable" people and modernize the nation.

HOLLOW FOLK

"They didn't want something that looked good. They wanted to show the worst side. They took pictures. Well, you've seen them. I know why they do it. You see, movies are made about the South. They'll be hillbillies and the rough people of the South, when you see the movies. And, well, people outside the South were viewing this community here. If it had been all spic and span and beautiful buildings, well, it wouldn't have been interesting to anybody."

This quote comes from a man who was interviewed by historians in the 1970s. He's describing a photograph taken by Lewis Hine of a school that he and my great-grandfather attended. My maternal great-grandfather was born in Loyston, Tennessee, in 1896. In the 1930s, Hine accepted a commission from the federal government to photograph Loyston residents before the government seized the land to facilitate the construction of rural development projects. The 1920s and 1930s became a critical decade in the construction of the "mountain white," a peculiar specimen thought to stubbornly resist social and even genetic progress. A new class of reformers deployed both visual and graphic images of white Appalachians to demonstrate the dangers of clinging to the past in an age of what the government hoped would be unprecedented modernization.

Hine, best known for his photographs that exposed the horrors of child labor, was not the only photographer commissioned to document the poor. The government employed a fleet of photographers, many through the Farm Security Administration (FSA). This form of visual cataloging complemented the agency's aim to resettle individuals living on "sub-marginal" land as part of a larger New Deal effort to modernize America. The government justified its actions in the name of progress and leveraged the consolidated power of the federal government to modernize the rural poor by force if necessary.

Hine worked directly for the Tennessee Valley Authority (TVA), an agency best known for creating government-owned power generating facilities. Most of Loyston proper is now at the bottom of a man-made lake—sometimes called the Loyston Sea—created by the TVA's Norris Dam project in 1936. My great-grandfather's land, however, was not submerged. Finding itself with surplus land, the government transferred ownership to the state of Tennessee for the creation of a state park at the site of the new lake. This was consistent with the government's broad aim to put sub-marginal land into the service of the public good.

The problem, of course, was that the government had the sole authority to determine the definition of "sub-marginal." Many residents, like the farmer quoted above, believed that the government, through selective photographic documentation and biased sociological studies, intentionally created a narrative that suited its purpose. My family was fortunate. Rural developers, photographers, and a new class of sociologists found them uninteresting on the whole and they simply relocated, without the promised assistance, to a community several miles away. Beyond Tennessee, some families met a much darker fate.

The FSA's fleet of photographers produced social documentation of enormous cultural significance. We are all familiar, for example, with Dorothea Lange's photographs of dust bowl migrants, and many brilliant photographers honed their skills with the FSA. Gordon Parks, a magnetic African American photographer, credited it with forcing him to "take a hard look backward at black history; to realize the burdens of those who had lived through it." This experience, Parks remarked, made him "much better prepared to face up to that history yet to be made."

Several of the subjects of FSA photographs became symbolic of their particular historical moment. Lange's "migrant mother," Florence Owens Thompson, became a visual representation of the strength of motherhood in the wake of enormous social upheaval. The African American cleaner, Ella Watson, the subject of Parks's *American Gothic*, became a symbolic representation of the unequal treatment of Black Americans during an age of progress.

Less is known about the subjects of Arthur Rothstein's first assignment with the FSA. Rothstein would later become a prolific photographer with tenures at *Look* and *Parade* magazines, but in 1936 he was twenty-one years old and among the first photographers sent on assignment by Roy Stryker, the head of the FSA's photographic unit. Rothstein's assignment was to document families living in Virginia's Shenandoah Valley, soon-to-be-evicted for the construction of a new national park.

Momentum to establish a national park in the area had existed for some time. The government authorized Shenandoah National Park in 1926, much to the enthusiasm of local Virginian businessmen and politicians, but progress on construction moved slowly because approximately five hundred families lived at the designated site. The state began to slowly acquire the necessary land through eminent domain, and in 1928, Virginia passed the Blanket Condemnation Act, which streamlined the state's acquisition of the 200,000 acres slated to become national park land.

Much like projects in the Tennessee Valley, the government framed the relocation of farmers as a benevolent process that would move residents geographically, but also temporally, from the nineteenth to the twentieth century. As you might imagine, then, expert opinion that confirmed this perception was in high demand.

The passage of the Condemnation Act brought many strangers with cameras to the Shenandoah Valley. Surveyors, social workers, academics, doctors, and photographers arrived to assess the residents and initiate the eviction process. In 1933, journalist Thomas Henry and University of Chicago sociologist Mandel Sherman released *Hollow Folk*, a book that purported to be a sociological study of the very people the government aimed to displace.

Their work largely follows a pattern of casting mountaineers as a primitive, isolated, and backwards people with a homogenous white ethnic identity and monoculture degraded through idleness and inbreeding. They write, "Social evolution presumably still goes on but so slowly do groups go forward under their own power that no movement can be discerned through generations." These less evolved individuals, the experts argued, could only be saved through the intervention of outsiders.

Henry and Sherman were assisted by the state's social workers, who helped them order the residents of the Shenandoah Valley into discrete geographical family units—the "hollows" of *Hollow Folk*—which they then scaled from most evolved to least evolved. They designated "Colvin Hollow," their quasi-fictitious name for Corbin Hollow, as the least evolved and most degraded.

Henry and Sherman, with no small amount of assistance from area social worker Miriam Sizer, described the residents of Colvin Hollow as living in primitive squalor, subsisting on a diet of weeds and small vermin, and overrun with illegitimate children. According to the two writers, these individuals knew little of the "outside world" and did not include in their basic vocabulary more modern words like "post office."

The ghosts of Henry and Sherman would like you to know that they were not eugenicists. That really doesn't matter, however, because eugenicists loved their work, filled as it was with lurid descriptions of white mountaineers' degraded "pioneer stock." Virginia was already at the forefront of the American eugenics movement thanks to the efforts of the Eugenics Records Office in Cold Spring Harbor, New York. The New York collective helped Virginia's politicians draft sterilization and racial integrity laws. In 1927 the fruits of their labor blossomed when the infamous Supreme Court case *Buck v. Bell* effectively legalized compulsory eugenic sterilization nationwide, which was practiced in Virginia until 1979.

According to Charles Davenport, the director of the Eugenics Record Office, Virginia's mountains were filled with mongrels of "a combination of the worst traits, a badly put together people." Many individuals thought to fit that description, like Carrie Buck, ended up at the Virginia State Colony for Epileptics and Feebleminded, where they were sterilized to, in the words of Supreme Court Justice Oliver Wendell Holmes, "prevent our being swamped with incompetence."

Into this environment stepped Arthur Rothstein, objective documentarian. Or was he? In 2011, Rothstein's work in the Shenandoah Valley became the subject of Richard Knox Robinson's film *Rothstein's First Assignment*. Robinson, himself a photographer, saw in Rothstein's photographs striking parallels to the narrative embedded in *Hollow Folk*. Rothstein extensively photographed, for example, the residents of "Colvin Hollow," including the mother of four illegitimate children who so captivated *Hollow Folk*'s authors.

Robinson suggests it was as if Rothstein used descriptions of subjects in *Hollow Folk* to guide his photographic eye, a not-unlikely crutch for a new photographer to use. Ignoring the presence and evictions of more "modern" residents who owned gas stations and restaurants, Rothstein delivered a photographic portfolio that shored up a narrative of the Shenandoah Valley as a place forgotten by time and progress.

Curiously, the mountaineers identified by both Rothstein and the authors of *Hollow Folk* as the most degenerate lived in the area of the Shenandoah Valley closest to developed areas of the future national park, where wealthy businessmen hoped to accelerate evictions to begin the expansion and new construction of vacation resorts. Many of them even worked at the Skyland Resort, which hoped to offer luxury accommodation to visitors of the new park.

What became of these mountaineers following their evictions was not widely known until Robinson set his documentary in motion. Although the government successfully relocated some mountaineers, others were destined for the Colony. This process appears to have begun during the writing of *Hollow Folk*, during which time the authors had frequent contact with area physicians and social workers.

Roy Sexton, an area doctor, wrote to Horace Albright, the Director of the National Park Service, "After the survey is done, we'll Colonize the worst of the bunch"—a sinister play on the eugenics institution's abbreviated name. Robinson found that the state authorized the institutionalization of at least eleven members of the family that populated "Colvin Hollow" at the Colony, nine of them children. Rothstein was present when social workers took two children away for institutionalization, photographing them just days prior.

In the early 1990s, the National Park Service funded a series of archaeological studies of the Shenandoah Valley. One focused on the settlement sites vacated by evicted residents. In Corbin Hollow, archaeologists found mass-produced furniture and toys, modern medicines, records, specialized farm equipment, shoes, an assortment of diningware, and even an automobile.

The most moving discovery, to me, was a Maxfield Parrish calendar for 1931. Parrish was a particularly striking illustrator known for his modern and vibrant colors, who often incorporated innovative drawing techniques to give his illustrations a three-dimensional feel. He was, in other words, an artist of his time, and the residents of Corbin Hollow decorated their home with his art because, contrary to belief, they were people of their time as well.

And with that we have our first example of the strange bond between up-and-comers on the Appalachia circuit and salivating eugenicists. And it will keep happening. Kelli Haywood, the Public Affairs Director of Whitesburg, Kentucky, radio station WMMT, recently argued that people in Appalachia dislike J.D. Vance because he "airs our dirty laundry." For me, this couldn't be further from the truth. I don't dislike Vance because I get embarrassed when he talks about "hillbilly culture." I dislike him because I think about children stolen from their parents. I think about white nationalist flyers that proclaim, "Appalachia is white, Scots-Irish, proud."

But the combination of dirty laundry and Whitesburg makes a nice set up for the next section, where we'll meet Vance's predecessor, Harry Caudill, a genteel lawyer from Whitesburg who showed the problems of Appalachia to the world and ultimately came to advocate for very disturbing solutions to them.

THE (RE) DISCOVERY OF APPALACHIA

Before 2016, the last time the nation took such an obsessive interest in West Virginia's politics was in 1960, when John F. Kennedy and Hubert Humphrey did battle during the state's Democratic primary. Kennedy had had a promising but unconvincing first primary result in Wisconsin in April—his win came courtesy of the state's substantial Catholic population—and West Virginia was next.

Kennedy campaigned throughout the entire state and by most accounts developed a genuine attachment to the people there, whom he often commended for their resilience in the face of economic distress. The people of West Virginia, in turn, awarded Kennedy with a victory in the state's primary. His win in a state with a small Catholic population helped convince the Democratic establishment that he could be a viable presidential candidate and the rest, as they say, is history.

Images captured during Kennedy's presidential campaign stops in West Virginia left an enduring impression on the nation. As Ronald Eller writes, "Kennedy's visible alarm at the conditions of the Mountain State and the attention given to economic issues in the presidential campaign lured dozens of journalists in the months that followed the election. Stories of human tragedy, personal struggle, cruel injustice, and heroic perseverance abounded in Appalachia and provided grist for a growing media mill of articles about poverty in America."

In August 1960, Julius Duscha wrote in the *Washington Post*, "Much of the Southern Appalachians is as underdeveloped, when compared with the affluence of the rest of the nation, as the newly independent countries of Africa." His essay, "A Long Trail of Misery Winds the Proud Hills," hinted at what would become a decidedly Cold War-era twist on long-standing narratives of Appalachian otherness: Appalachia as a third world within the heart of America.

This twist applied a particular post-war logic to the problems of Appalachia. If America was willing, this logic implied, to use its abundant wealth to help develop African countries striking out from their colonial pasts, then shouldn't it apply the same effort and offer the same assistance to poor Appalachians at home? The myth of Appalachia as homogenous and white went far in capturing the attention of the nation. Photographers, journalists, and reformers stuck closely to this myth in capturing stories of an "other America" that would help fuel what would become the nation's War on Poverty.

Into this moment came Kentucky writer and attorney Harry Caudill, a born and bred Appalachian spokesperson who had a storied career as the voice of a misunderstood region. In 1967, Caudill helped prosecute Hobart Ison for the murder of Hugh O'Connor, but in the early 1960s, he was at work on his exposé of coal mining, which he first published in 1962 in the *Atlantic* with the provocative title "The Rape of the Appalachians."

Strip mining—the excavation of coal through the surface of soil and rock rather than via subterranean means—had recently become an established method of extraction in eastern Kentucky. This had resulted in broad changes to the landscape and labor practices in coal communities. Environmental destruction became more rampant. Strip mining also required fewer miners, which led to widespread unemployment. Communities and landowners attempted to curb this practice through the courts, arguing that strip mining was an "unusual and wholly unforeseen method" of extraction inconsistent with the terms of existing coal leases. The courts sided with coal companies, and Caudill went on the warpath.

"The cumulative effects of the wrecking of a coal-filled mountain stagger the imagination," he wrote in "The Rape of the Appalachians." His article largely attends to the realities ushered forth by strip mining, including its toxic effects on vegetation, waterways, wildlife, and people. He spared no restraint in holding "absentee corporations" accountable for "the physical destruction of the land and the abject impoverishment of its people," labeling the coal industry's control of eastern Kentucky a relic of a "laissez-faire century." Caudill quickly expanded his article into a book, which became 1963's *Night Comes to the Cumberlands: A Biography of a Distressed Area*.

Just a year prior, socialist writer Michael Harrington had released an influential study of poverty, *The Other America: Poverty in the United States*. The book primed the nation and its politicians to seek out previously unacknowledged communities on the brink of economic annihilation. Dwight Macdonald, a cultural critic, summed up the collective response to Harrington's work in the *New Yorker* by writing, "In the last year we seem to have suddenly awakened, rubbing our eyes like Rip Van Winkle, to the fact that massive poverty exists." The extent of poverty, Macdonald commented, "is difficult to believe in the United States of 1963, but one has to make an effort, and it is now being made."

Caudill became the spokesperson for Appalachia and a translator of white mountain poverty to the nation. *Night Comes to the Cumberlands* became a commercial success and the *New York Times* and other influential publications sent reporters to Kentucky to confirm Caudill's descriptions of the region. Caudill often relied on romantic and problematic notions of Appalachia and its people to give his stories of regional exploitation their bite. He enjoyed the spotlight, taking visiting reporters on "poverty tours" near his Whitesburg home.

Almost everything about Caudill's persona—his middle-class profession, his wholesome family life, and his eloquence—challenged dominant perceptions of the region. This is precisely why the press found him irresistible. The press embraced Caudill, much like Vance, because he could be both of the people and above the people. At his best, Caudill was a formidable enemy of the coal industry, leveraging his influence to expose and arrest the destruction of land by corporations. But he could also be vicious toward the poor, particularly after federal assistance came to the region.

Both Caudill and Vance set themselves to the task of drawing the nation's attention away from social unrest and racial inequality at a particular moment in time and refocusing it instead on the conditions of white poverty. For Caudill, that moment was the War on Poverty, the popular name for the flurry of legislation adopted by the Johnson administration in the mid-1960s designed to combat both urban and rural poverty. Architects of this legislation intended solutions to poverty to be race-neutral, but the administration's emphasis on Appalachian poverty provided many social reformers with problems that seemed, to their relief, far distant from those entwined with the civil rights movement.

Kennedy's commitment to addressing Appalachia's poverty became part of his legacy, adopted by the Johnson administration as part of the Great Society agenda, when the new president declared "an unconditional war on poverty in America." In April 1964, Johnson traveled to Appalachia to fulfill Kennedy's pledge to revisit the area. His "poverty tour" also included stops in Chicago and Pittsburgh, but the press images from Johnson's stop in Martin County, Kentucky, provided the public relations magic that transformed the War on Poverty from a series of related legislation to an agenda with a deep moral purpose.

Black and white photographs of children playing in bare shacks, restless with hunger, and tended to by parents aged beyond their years, captivated the nation. *Life* magazine featured twelve pages of these images in the January 31, 1964, issue under the title "The Valley of Poverty." *Life* intended the images to serve as an indictment of "a wealthy nation's indifference." "Their homes are shacks without plumbing or sanitation," the article explained, "Their landscape is a man-made desolation of corrugated hills and hollows laced with polluted streams. The people, themselves—often disease-ridden and unschooled—are without jobs and even hope."

These images worked, much like *Elegy* works today, by offering middle-class white viewers a glimpse into a world that feels both familiar and alien. This world unburdens the white viewer from the fatigue of thinking critically about race, a mercy expressed in *Elegy* in its dismissal of the "racial prism." Poverty pictures allowed comfortable white Americans to consume the difference embedded in the images while believing they were engaging critically with pressing social issues. In 1964, this attention complemented the War on Poverty's logic and design.

When people asked Adam Yarmolinsky, one of Johnson's economic advisors, if the War on Poverty had a color, he responded, "Color it Appalachian if you are going to color it anything at all." Appalachian historian John Alexander Williams notes, "The youthful volunteers who staffed the anti-poverty offices and community actions programs of the Kennedy-Johnson years were, like the religious and benevolent workers of the last century, fleeing events in the lowland South, namely the rise of Black Power…the liberal television commentators and welfare bureaucrats who displayed Appalachian poverty to the nation took obvious relish in the white skins and blue eyes of the region's hungry children."

The press rarely used images of poor Black Appalachians in their exposés of regional poverty. Public support for the War on Poverty depended on getting white, middle-class Americans to care about poverty, and projections of white poverty worked best in this regard. This led to an overabundance of images and stories about white poverty and, according to Ronald Eller, "helped establish a pattern of critical but superficial commentary that would sustain the image of Appalachia as a problem area for years to come." Sound familiar?

Reformers, photographers, the press, and politicians flocked to Appalachia to find the form of poverty they needed and wanted to see. The peculiar privilege of serving as the face of poverty had benefits—the Appalachian Regional Commission is in many ways a success story. But it also created a new consumer demand for sensational stories that helped the nation form opinions about who they imagined the deserving and undeserving poor to be. The War on Poverty did not succeed in coaxing the nation from its prejudices, but it proved that the poverty industry—capturing visual or graphic images of poverty, serving as a politician tasked with administering federal aid—could be profitable.

Although attitudes toward Appalachian poverty were highly problematic, they often appeared benevolent compared to attitudes toward African American poverty. The Moynihan Report of 1965, to use just one example, remains a particularly searing, biased, and unfair indictment of African American families. The Department of Labor commissioned the report from sociologist Daniel Patrick Moynihan and intended to use his findings in the development of War on Poverty economic policy. The resulting study, *The Negro Family: The Case for National Action*, is a remarkable example of the culture of poverty framework in action.

Moynihan concluded that the foundations of the nation's African American family were so weak, there was nothing but a "tangle of pathology" in place of a social structure. Every quality that was idealized in the world white middle-class families inhabited was absent in Black families. Black fathers were either not present or emasculated by bread-winning Black mothers, a perverse phenomenon that primed young children, particularly boys, for a life of low ambition, drugs, and crime. Moynihan's report had little utility for the Johnson administration after civil rights activists denounced it. But conservative politicians and intellectuals resurrected it in the 1970s and 80s. They used Moynihan's findings—now stacked against a decade's worth of social trends ripe for malleable interpretation—to argue that public assistance programs did more to undermine Black family life than improve it.

You might be asking, "Why does *Hillbilly Elegy* sound kind of like the Moynihan Report?" One reason is that white Appalachians became *persona non grata* after the War on Poverty failed. The nation began to see them as individuals who had absorbed an unprecedented amount of federal aid and done nothing with it except continue to be poor. Hillbillies had wasted taxpayer money, a cardinal sin that placed them in the ranks of the undeserving poor, an often racialized category that nevertheless has always welcomed white individuals thought to be, as Caudill once said, the "dregs" of society.

The other reason *Elegy* sounds like the Moynihan Report is that the white people who are outspoken in their beliefs about the culture of poverty simply don't count poor white Appalachians as part of their tribe. As *Elegy* makes clear, it's satisfying to imagine us as a different culture, even a different genetic specimen, than "good" white people. Just look at headlines proclaiming us to be "members of America's forgotten tribe" if you want to understand how easy it is to naturalize this outlook. Both of these asinine positions, unfortunately, came to reshape Caudill's thinking about Appalachia and its problems.

The same year that Moynihan completed his report, a new leader in the American eugenics movement emerged. "Is the quality of the U.S. population declining?" asked Stanford scientist William Shockley in a November 1965 edition of *U.S. News and World Reports*. After clarifying that he was not speaking of individuals who are "substantially retarded" and do "very little breeding," Shockley explained, "The real cause of worry is people of somewhat higher ability but still, say, near the bottom of the population in the ability to reason and plan ahead...not only are they dull but they need help to survive. Most cannot advance and some are a threat to other people."

Asked what role genetics played in high incidences of "Negroes on crime and welfare relief rolls," Shockley answered that "if you look at the median Negro I.Q., it almost always turns out to be not as good as the median white I.Q....is there an imbalance in the reproduction of superior and inferior strains? This we do not know." With the help of wealthy benefactors, Shockley would make it his mission to find out.

The *L.A. Times* wrote of him, "Shockley strayed well beyond the confines of established genetics into the shoals of eugenics. He suggested that welfare and relief programs prevented natural selection from killing off 'the bottom of the population': 'with improvements to technology…inferior strains have increased chances for survival and reproduction at the same time birth control has tended to reduce family size among superior elements.'"

By the 1970s, Shockley had been largely disowned by the mainstream scientific community. Although he continued to advance his theories, he was incredibly sensitive to accusations that he was a racist. In 1974, for example, he debated the African American psychiatrist Frances Cress Welsing. It was a mortifying experience for Shockley in which he attempted to refute any racist underpinnings in his obsession with eugenics. He preferred to label himself a "raceologist," an objective observer of the differences between races.

It's here that we re-discover Caudill, disillusioned by the failures of the War on Poverty. Rather than stimulating the ambition of Appalachians, Caudill believed that a decade of government assistance had only rendered mountain people more complacent and dependent on social welfare. He became convinced this dependency had something to do with their defective genes. In *Night Comes to the Cumberlands,* shared ethnic ancestry within Appalachia gave the region a sense of romantic and noble mystery. A decade later it was, to Caudill, a source of the region's woe.

BRAIN DRAIN

Caudill began to follow Shockley's career closely, clipping newspaper articles about his work. In 1974, he sent Shockley a fan letter in which he confessed, "The poverty that is associated with our region is accompanied by passivity and dependence and

I see no present hope for allaying it. I have come full circle in my thinking and have reluctantly concluded that the poverty that called into being the Appalachian Regional Commission is largely genetic in origin and is largely irreducible."

By that point in his career, Shockley was openly advocating coercive sterilization for the "genetically unfit." It appears that he saw in Caudill's letter the potential to once again attempt to mitigate his racism by examining dysgenics, the spread of defective genes, in a predominately white population. Hoping to pilot a study that would legitimize his research and lead to federal funding for his sterilization program, Shockley agreed to meet Caudill in Kentucky to discuss the genetic fitness of white Appalachians.

The two men called their meeting the "Whitesburg Conference." It took place at Caudill's home and members of Shockley's inner circle attended, including J.W. Kirkpatrick, a Ku Klux Klan financier, and Robert Travis Osborne, a segregationist. Their agenda, outlined earlier by Kirkpatrick, was to establish a pilot program in Whitesburg to "test a limited number of people representative of a group of a couple of generations of mountaineers with apparent low intelligence to determine if dysgenics is taking place." There seemed to be little doubt among participants that the study would yield their desired results. If all went according to plan, Kirkpatrick shared, "the sterilization plan will be an outgrowth of the pilot program and can be implemented at some point after the pilot program has been completed and evaluated."

"As I remember Harry Caudill repeated several times his grave concern that welfare programs in Appalachia which were intended to rehabilitate the people into more productive members of society were not going to be fruitful because of the brain drain," Kilpatrick wrote. "If extensive research confirms that observation, then there should be drastic revisions in the projects for welfare and rehabilitation now being carried out...as well as further consideration to Dr. Shockley's proposal of sterilization on a voluntary basis for money."

After the conference, Caudill repeated his recommendations to Shockley in a follow-up letter. Apparently the people of Appalachia, although deemed unfit by Caudill, were intelligent enough to understand the often sinister purposes of intelligence testing because much of Caudill's advice concerned how to not raise suspicions about the true nature of the study. "I suggested that we avoid the term 'intelligence test' simply because by doing so we might avoid some critical and troublesome newspaper publicity," he wrote, identifying a particular county where people "are breeding down to idiocy." He offered suggestions that sound very close to an endorsement of bribery to bring school officials on board by engaging them as paid consultants. This was, in essence, how much of the research in *Hollow Folk* took place as well.

Fortunately, funding for the study and subsequent sterilization programs did not materialize and Shockley and Caudill never met again. For some time, however, Caudill continued to correspond with Shockley and other eugenicists, including Nathaniel Hirsch. Caudill wrote to Hirsch months after the Whitesburg Conference that "during the Johnson years when anti-poverty programs were in vogue I once told a federal official that the best way to fight poverty would be to move an army camp into the region. My theory was that the soldiers would get the mountain girls pregnant to the everlasting benefit of the region as a whole. I still think the suggestion was sound." One can believe he did indeed make such a remark. *Night Comes to the Cumberlands* is full of sexist descriptions of "rangy, narrow-minded, stubborn, and clannish" women who "continued to multiply with all the astounding efficiency which has marked their history in the Southern hills."

It's difficult to know what to make of Caudill's early work in the region given his open association with eugenicists in his later life. Much in his correspondence with these individuals seems to indicate that he always felt this bias toward poor white mountaineers and simply adopted a more modern language, provided by dysgenics, to express his views. It isn't hard to locate shadows of these beliefs in his older work. The *Lexington-Herald Ledger* revealed much of this correspondence publicly, drawn from Caudill's personal papers housed at the University of Kentucky, during the fiftieth anniversary year of *Night Comes to the Cumberlands* in 2013. Caudill passed away in 1990, but his wife, Anne, called the publication of the correspondence a deliberate attempt to "besmirch" her husband's legacy by emphasizing a "minuscule" episode from his past.

Anne Caudill writes, "After further correspondence, he became dubious about the direction of the discourse and dropped it." To put her framework in modern terms, Anne Caudill argued that her husband was simply engaging in the "marketplace of ideas" and, as part of his civic responsibility to his people, felt inclined to cast his net widely for solutions to their problems. Although she knew her husband better than we ever will or could, it must be noted that Harry Caudill wouldn't be the last person to deflect a willingness to elevate problematic and dangerous theories in the service of encouraging self-help.

Shockley died an embarrassment in 1989, but certain aspects of his work and legacy live on. An organization called The Pioneer Fund provided financial assistance to Shockley's non-profit Foundation for Research and Education of Eugenics and Dysgenics and publicized his work in white nationalist circles. Despite this wealthy benefactor, Shockley conducted surprisingly little scientific research and overspent his research grants on free speech crusades.

In the 1990s, The Pioneer Fund came under public scrutiny after it was revealed that a number of the sources used by Charles Murray and Richard Herrnstein for *The Bell Curve* were researchers affiliated with the organization. "Many of *The Bell Curve*'s most important assertions which establish casual links between IQ and social behavior, and IQ and race, are derived partially or totally from the *Mankind Quarterly*—Pioneer Fund scholarly circle," wrote Charles Lane in the December 1994 issue of the *New York Review of Books*.

Even without this direct link it would not be difficult to place Shockley as a not-distant intellectual ancestor of Charles Murray. Murray, who once burned a cross during what he described as a teenage prank, maintained the soundness of his borrowed research despite its provenance. The scientific community widely condemned *The Bell Curve* and Murray left the academy to become a pubic intellectual on the subject of race science.

The *New York Times* wrote in 1994 that "Shockley receives only one guarded paragraph in the 845 pages of *The Bell Curve*. Yet his old pronouncements are everywhere...The more elegantly written *Bell Curve* has the same drift. Shockley bequeathed its authors their self-congratulatory tone as well: He boasted about raising 'questions that are usually swept under the rug' as they do about taboos. Mr. Murray and Mr. Herrnstein also emulate Shockley by asserting expertise in academic disciplines (like genetics) outside their own and by protesting too much against those who might accuse them of making a fetish of race."

BRAIN DRAIN REDUX

And this is where we pick up the story of Vance again, sitting across the stage from Charles Murray at the American Enterprise Institute in October 2016. Our second example of this strange bond quickly transitions to the third. The camaraderie performed by the pair was, in some ways, an outgrowth of their mutual appreciation. Vance cited Murray's *Coming Apart* approvingly in *Elegy* and often in interviews, and Murray found *Elegy* riveting as well. The occasion of their talk was an hourlong conversation about the decline of the white working class, and Vance appeared eager to tell Murray what he clearly wanted to hear about the genetic dimensions of this decline.

Over laughs and jokes, the pair discussed their "pretty clean Scots-Irish blood" while getting to the heart of what "hillbilly culture" actually is. "It's worth noting," Vance explained, "that if you look at ethnographic studies of this area you find that the Scots-Irish are disproportionately represented in this area of the country…so there's definitely a sort of ethnic component to what's going on in these areas." He continued, "There's something to be said for the fact that Scots-Irish culture is both unique and regionally distinct but it's also spread pretty far and wide." Murray, who in the darkest corners of his brain still likes to believe he's a social scientist, nodded and smiled at this conflicting package of attributes that wouldn't pass a freshman essay—regionally distinct but spread far and wide!—as if it was the truest fact he'd ever heard.

Murray, who also claims Scots-Irish ancestry, was quick to point out, "and our leading characteristics though, which I learned long before I read *Hillbilly Elegy*, is being drunk and violent." More laughs. A week after the incident at Middlebury College, in which student protestors shut down Murray's lecture, Vance made it a point to credit him for his theories on "brain drain" in his *New York Times* op-ed about why he was moving back to Ohio.

John Thomason notes that "Vance cites racist-thinking far more directly than even his critics have indicated. The very first end-note references Razib Khan, a writer who the *New York Times* dropped as a regular science contributor after *Gawker* revealed his 'history with racist, far-right online publications.' Charles Murray…the most famous racial determinist in contemporary America is cited approvingly." It's a chilling exercise to consider why individuals who are happy to deconstruct Black life down to the smallest data-point and to savage critics who disagree find J.D. Vance to be a savant in cultural studies, a field coincidentally held in poor regard by most conservative thinkers.

There are many authors who have written about the people and problems of Appalachia and similar environments who don't have eugenicists for pen-pals and mentors. Some of them even anchor frank discussions of social problems within moving personal stories. Otis Trotter's *Keeping Heart*, a memoir about growing up poor, sick, and Black in Appalachian Ohio springs to mind, as does Rick Bragg's *All Over but the Shoutin'*. *The Glass Castle* by Jeannette Walls is the story of a dysfunctional West Virginian family and finding the courage to leave. Linda Tate, in *Power in the Blood*, tells of the re-discovery of her Cherokee roots, and *Creeker,* by Linda Scott DeRosier, is yet another memoir about coming of age in Appalachia.

"No book about Appalachia has gotten this much attention since Harry Caudill's *Night Comes to the Cumberlands* was published in 1963," the *Daily Yonder* wrote of *Elegy.* Amazon tries to sell me *Elegy* if I view the page for *Night Comes* (and vice versa), and instructors are now pairing the texts together in their Introduction to Appalachian Studies courses. Imagine what it feels like to understand that if someone decides to purchase a book about Appalachia, there's a 100 percent chance they'll be recommended not one but two books used by their authors to win the esteem of white supremacists and eugenicists.

Living with this fatigue is real. In the age of *Hillbilly Elegy*, a book applauded by the *National Review* for proving that signs of white distress "have gone neglected as LGBTQ identity politics and Black Lives Matter antics" have monopolized the nation's attention, we're told to be grateful that Vance has returned Appalachia to the nation's conscience. But I don't want Appalachia to be used as a siphon to suck attention away from LGBTQ politics and Black Lives Matter, movements that also flourish here. I don't want to lose race in discussions of class. I don't want to keep talking about "brain drain" when millions of smart, capable, and good people still call the region home. I don't want anything that Vance could ever give the region, which works out, because he's far more interested in taking.

A neutral observer might say that the best course of action is simply to ignore the *Elegy* phenomenon as best we can. You must understand that isn't possible. Vance is in our schools, our libraries. He is at our graduations. He is on our timelines and in our newspaper. He is a member of our faculties, with new honorary degrees. He's like the monster from *It Follows*. The best we can do, as community columnist Jillean McCommons suggests in the *Lexington-Herald Ledger*, is "turn that anger into your next writing project. Write about your people. Tell your story. Answer with pen and pad."

Last year, my alma mater, a state school outside of Appalachia, selected *Elegy* as required reading for all incoming freshmen and paired its selection with a financial arrangement with photographer Shelby Lee Adams to sell his Appalachian poverty pictures. Known for posed and stylized black and white portrait work of mountain families, Adams has made a career photographing the poor. Among Appalachians, he is controversial. Like many photographers before him, including Arthur Rothstein, he favors images of poor, often disabled, individuals in contexts that he frequently manipulates.

Adams often photographs the same families over time, and has developed what he presents as an insider status among his impoverished subjects despite his own solidly middle-class upbringing and training at the Cleveland Institute of Art. His most forceful claim to this status appears in his *Appalachian Lives* through the ghost of Hobart Ison, the man who murdered Hugh O'Connor.

Among the photographs, Adams tells a story. One day he finds himself down a holler in Kentucky, photographing a family and their trailer. As he works, the owner of the property—this time, a woman—arrives and orders him to leave. In this version of the "stranger-with-a-camera" story, Adams has a less heated exchange with the property owner, who nevertheless menaces him by asking him if knows what people do to nosy photographers in Letcher County. Not only is he aware, Adams defiantly tells the property owner that Hobart Ison—whom he refers to as Hobert Isom in his text—is his third cousin.

Adams's subjects become active participants in his version of the legend by helping drive away the property owner so he can continue taking their pictures. In their conversation after the encounter, Adams reports that the family provided its blessing to sell their images "for a thousand dollars apiece," confronting and ultimately dismissing in smug fashion questions of exploitation in Adams's arrangements with his subjects. My former university insisted that Adams's work "is the photographic analog of J.D. Vance's book *Hillbilly Elegy*…the author and the photographer tell corresponding stories through different means."

This is true, but not in the way that my alma mater insists that it is. The shared story and analogues at work are not about people, but about power. It reflects how credibility falls easily to those given the privilege of defining *who* or *what* Appalachian is. It also shows the rewards that fall to individuals, universally men and exclusively white, regardless of the company they keep. It is the power to grant yourself permission for continued exploitation of vulnerable subjects. It is the power to have your work selected as emblematic of a cultural moment by individuals and organizations that didn't care one iota about Appalachia until their gaze could fill the region with pathologies.

Vance is a well-educated person of means with a powerful platform who has chosen to accept a considerable amount of fame and wealth to become the spokesperson for a region. Since he is such an enormous fan of personal responsibility, I am thrilled to hold him responsible for his asinine beliefs and associations. Appalachian blogger Kelli Haywood, in her essays on *Elegy*, objects to the individuals who claim that Vance isn't authentically Appalachian because he migrated outside the region. I don't give a damn about geography, but I'll note that Vance has transcended one of the most authentically Appalachian experiences of them all: watching someone with tired ideas about race and culture get famous by selling cheap stereotypes about the region.

PART III
LAND, JUSTICE, PEOPLE

In 1967, the sheriff of Pike County, Kentucky, ordered a raid on the home of community organizers Karen and Joseph Mulloy, a young couple affiliated with a number of anti-poverty and anti-coal programs. To the delight of law enforcement and the county's political elite, the raid unearthed "a Communist library out of this world" that included Adam Smith's *The Wealth of Nations* and Karl Marx's *Das Kapital*. The sheriff, the appropriately named Perry Justice, ordered the arrest of Joseph, his neighbor Alan McSurely, and his friend Carl Braden for sedition against the government of Pike County.

This was the second time that Braden found himself charged with sedition in Kentucky. In 1954, he and his wife Anne helped purchase a home for an African American couple, Andrew and Charlotte Wade, in Louisville. The swift backlash, which included an attempt by white neighbors to dynamite the home, prompted Braden's arrest. The pretext? They were attempting to overthrow the commonwealth by igniting a race war. The court convicted Carl Braden and sentenced him to a term of fifteen years. He served eighteen months in prison, and forty-two days in solitary confinement, before the Supreme Court, ruling on a case in Pennsylvania, determined that charges of sedition were only applicable in federal matters, not state or local. During the 1954 trial, the Bradens lost approximately 800 books, seized by law enforcement, and spent $40,000 in legal fees.

Over a decade later, Perry Justice alleged that the Mulloys and McSurelys, with the assistance of Braden, were attempting to "take over Pike County from the power structure and put it in the hands of the poor" by using mountain people and anti-poverty workers to "promote causes aimed at downgrading and maybe overthrowing the Government." The commonwealth charged them with "teaching or advocating criminal syndicalism against the state," an ambiguous legal tactic most often reserved to harass labor unions and their supporters. Although Pike County officials knew sedition charges were unconstitutional, the Mulloys and McSurelys were indeed attempting to help poor individuals in the mountains seize power from the wealthy. In other words, they were engaging in one of the finest and oldest Appalachian traditions.

One of the most offensive "Trump Country" essays I have encountered came courtesy of Kevin Baker in the March 2017 issue of the *New Republic*. It's a painfully smug attempt to effect a kind of *gotcha* by juxtaposing historic Appalachian labor uprisings against our presumed present complacency. *Look at how far the radical have fallen*, Baker seems to argue, setting Blair Mountain insurrections against the tepid and polite applause for coal interests at a televised Bernie Sanders rally. But we are not accountable to Baker's narrow definition of radical, which nods in limp recognition at men with guns, but excludes individuals like the Mulloys, McSurelys, and the Bradens.

A flaw of popular narratives of Appalachia is the willingness of authors to describe destruction and social decline in lurid detail while remaining wholly uninterested in the people who challenged it. To the *National Review*, Appalachia is the "white ghetto," a place filled with "the unemployed, the dependent, and the addicted." To me, Appalachia is a battleground, where industry barons, social reformers, and workers wage a constant war that is passed down through generations, often reflecting inherited struggles that feel repeated and never-ending.

When I imagine our history, I see photographs. You might notice that visual cues populate this volume, which is an artifact of both my peculiar way of thinking and also of the frequency with which photographers, journalists, and visual artists come to document us. References to challenging ways of *seeing* or *looking at* Appalachia appear in many projects created *by* Appalachians as opposed to those that are *about* Appalachians. It is often second nature for many of us to inject the language of visual literacy into our work because we're accustomed to serving as passive subjects for others and ultimately just want to be seen as we truly are.

So like any good host, let me conclude our visit by dragging out our family photo album to show you Appalachia as I see it. Here is Anne Braden, dressed in black, with her neat pocketbook and tilted head at her husband's sedition trial. Here is Myles Horton, a labor and civil rights activist from Tennessee, flanked by Rosa Parks and Septima Clark. Here is Robert Payne, a disabled African American miner who helped lead one of the largest wildcat strikes in history as president of the Disabled Miners and Widows organization. Here is Eula Hall, with her big, teased hair and her finger pointed in the face of every bureaucrat that stood in her way. Here is Huey Perry, poised to lead a hundred-car-long funeral procession to mark the death of his community action group. Here are my grandparents, here are your grandparents. Here is Judy Bonds, fishing with her grandchildren after her shift at Pizza Hut, before she became the face of anti-mountaintop-removal activism. This is who we are. This is who we have been all this time.

TO SAVE THE LAND AND PEOPLE

There is a single figure in the photograph I see in my head that is otherwise cluttered with the artifacts of ruined land—slender and crooked branches, deep ravines—and industrial equipment. The figure is an elderly woman, sixty-six years old and aged even beyond that by poverty, with a dark-colored kerchief on her head and a walking stick by her side. She stands before a bulldozer with her head bowed.

She is sitting in the next frame. Depending on the angle of the photographer—Bill Strode working for the *Courier-Journal* out of Louisville—the bulldozer is still visible but so are trees ripped from the earth by their roots. In one image her kneeling frame even appears underwater because the shadows of equipment and the shadows of dead things engulf her small body.

The final frame is perhaps the last one Strode captured before police arrested him for documenting the woman's protest. A uniformed officer has his hands hooked beneath her arms. A man in a dark suit, looking wholly out of place on a ravaged mountain, supports her feet. She is limp. The middle of her body sags beneath the two men because, although she is light, she has forced them to carry her down a steep mountain.

This is how I see Ollie Combs, who in 1965 sat in front of the Caperton Coal Company's bulldozers to protest their abuse of her land. A legal loophole gave Caperton ownership of the minerals beneath Combs's land and the land surrounding it, and although she owned everything above ground, exploitive land deeds entitled coal companies to extract these minerals by any means necessary, including the destruction of her home and property. I see Ollie Combs in jail, on Thanksgiving, eating alone.

There is another image, uncaptured, that should haunt your memories. Testifying against coal companies in eastern Kentucky, young women described watching bulldozers rip through a family cemetery. Alice Sloan, a Kentucky-area educator, described how Bige Richie pleaded with the coal company to spare the grave of her child: "The bulldozer pushed over the hill and she begged them not to go through the graveyard. And she looked out there and there was her baby's coffin come rolling down the hill. One man said he wouldn't go through and push it down. The other said, 'Hell, I will,' and he took the bulldozer and went right on through."

The struggle to prevent the wholesale destruction of land by strip-mining coal companies in eastern Kentucky gave rise to the

Appalachian Group to Save the Land and People. This grassroots organization was established after an eighty-one-year-old preacher named Dan Gibson used armed resistance to route bulldozers off his family land in Knott County, Kentucky, in 1965. Ollie Combs was a member, as were many elderly Kentuckians who tried to protect the land while their children and grandchildren were fighting in Vietnam. Like coal companies, the Appalachian Group to Save the Land and People went about its business by any means necessary. It waged painfully slow legal challenges through the courts, but members also engaged in more militant forms of action and in illegal methods of protest such as industrial sabotage.

The fringe group Mountaintop Gun Club, for example, rented private surface land for $1 from concerned landowners. In return, the club established shooting ranges on threatened land in the hopes that the presence of armed individuals might deter coal companies from taking the land by force. Members of the Appalachian Group to Save the Land and People described parts of eastern Kentucky in the late 1960s as a war zone where armed residents faced off daily against coal operators.

Joseph Mulloy was among the young anti-poverty workers who joined forces with grassroots community groups, including the Appalachian Group to Save the Land and People. Many anti-poverty workers came to the region optimistic that a more efficient distribution of federal aid and resources would help win the War on Poverty. The region's political elites and local business leaders, however, benefitted from the uneven distribution of wealth. In the 1960s, Pike County had a population of just 5,000 people, most of them poor. But there were also over fifty millionaires who had been enriched by the coal industry.

Just before his arrest in the summer of 1967, Mulloy and his wife Karen joined a protest against the Puritan Coal Company to support an elderly farmer who, like Combs, had placed his body in the path of bulldozers. When the farmer won a legal battle to protect his land, Pike County's coal operators and political elites took their frustrations out on the Mulloys and orchestrated the arrest of the couple and their friends on charges law enforcement knew to be illegal. This was after other, more bureaucratic forms of harassment had failed, including revoking the Mulloy's car insurance and cutting off their utilities.

When the commonwealth could not proceed with charges against the Mulloys, it established the Kentucky Un-American Activities Committee to investigate, in a more general way, "activities of groups and organizations which have as their objective…the overthrow or destruction of the Commonwealth of Kentucky by force, violence, or other unlawful means." Kentucky's political elite intended the Un-American Activities Committee to intimidate young activists like the Mulloys and to destabilize the place that anti-poverty workers occupied in local communities.

In its intent and design, the Kentucky Un-American Activities Committee presented any opposition to the existing power structure—which at that time reflected political corruption of the highest order—as outside agitation. The Un-American Activities Committee concluded that the subversives were "outsiders that they brought in from all over the nation…and the local people resented them." It was certainly true that many young organizers came from outside the region during the War on Poverty, but they often told a different story about how radical action came to the mountains. According to many volunteers, mountain people radicalized them, not the other way around. One explained, "I felt like I was radicalized or politicized or whatever by the people who lived in the mountains themselves."

Rebellious activists didn't transplant radical action against corporate interests to the mountains. That radical action originated here. In 1968, a year after Kentucky succeeded in terminating the funding for many anti-poverty workers, four masked men ambushed the night watchman for the Round Mountain Coal Company in Leslie County, leaving him tied up and blindfolded in a vehicle. Four hours later, explosive charges, stolen from the company's own supply, detonated, destroying almost a million dollars' worth of heavy equipment. The saboteurs, although their identities were never discovered, were likely homegrown. They had intimate familiarity with the land and with mining equipment. Perhaps most significantly, they lived in a world where destruction of land was an accepted part of life.

FOR THE GOOD OF THE POOR AND COMMON PEOPLE

Another treasured image is a more recently taken photograph of my West Virginian friend Roger May with elderly community organizer Huey Perry. May is a prolific photographer who coordinated the *Looking at Appalachia* project, which aimed to "explore the diversity of Appalachia and establish a visual counterpoint" to stereotypical images of eternal white poverty. His project has introduced me to some of my favorite photographers, including Megan King, who documents Hispanic Appalachia, and Raymond Thompson, who photographs the journeys of families to visit their incarcerated relatives.

Perry looks a bit small next to May—to be fair, May is very tall—but to me, he's a giant. Perry, a former history teacher from Mingo County, West Virginia, put his teaching career on hold to fight the war on poverty in the 1960s by directing community action groups in the poorest part of the state, a struggle he documented in his memoir *They'll Cut Off Your Project: A Mingo County Chronicle*. Perry's memoir is an equally humorous and painful account of what the War on Poverty might have achieved but ultimately didn't. He tells a story that is similar to the drama that unfolded in eastern Kentucky as political corruption and the influence of corporate interests hijacked anti-poverty funding from the poor.

By their design, the anti-poverty programs that Perry administered acknowledged that existing avenues of support—from traditional forms of welfare like the Aid to Families with

Dependent Children of the Unemployed fund, to the efforts of elected representatives and the priorities of regional businesses— were insufficient to combat widespread structural poverty. Perry used the principles of community organizing to bring poor people together, and found these principles to be successful.

The War on Poverty's logic worked something like this. In Appalachia, it often happened that flooding caused by mining destroyed roads. Community residents would approach coal companies to ask permission to use their private access roads, requests that were universally denied. Community residents would would ask their political leaders for urgent assistance rebuilding their roads, requests that were universally denied. What the War on Poverty did was come to communities to rebuild roads. What the War on Poverty didn't do was help poor people deal with the fact that they lived in a world where those who hoarded wealth would rather see them starve than share. Perry tried to change that by rigging the War on Poverty to work directly for the people.

In Mingo County alone, Perry supported as many as twenty-six community action groups. Individually, these groups worked toward addressing problems with educational facilities, food scarcity, poor roads, voting rights, political transparency, and unemployment. Starting with Mingo's African American community, Perry and his staff formed community groups wherever locals were receptive to them. "Participation in a community group," he wrote, "afforded them security for the first time in their lives."

"A community action group would consist of low income citizens organized together to identify their problems and work toward possible solutions," he explained. "I feel it is necessary that we take our time and build an organization that involves the poor in the decisions as to what types of programs they want, rather than sit down and write up what we think they want." This was the ethic that fueled much of the logic of Appalachian grassroots activism and motivated young reformers during the War on Poverty—involving and integrating poor people into every aspect of community life and governance.

But there were problems. Mingo County's political establishment—both elected officials and businessmen who commanded political clout—often opposed this work. "In old England," one of Perry's staff commented, "if a king didn't like you, he would cut off your head. Now if they don't like you, they'll cut off your project!" Mingo's political establishment hoped it could do what elected officials and businessmen in neighboring McDowell County had done, which was to siphon off federal funding—as much as two million dollars—and use it for their own purposes, most often to buy votes or sweeten business arrangements to ensure patronage.

When people ask, "Why do Appalachians always vote against their own interests?" here we see that, historically, a very compelling and simple answer to that question was voter fraud.

For Perry, getting back to community didn't look like preaching the gospel of bootstrapping to the poor. It meant union building and mutual aid. It meant labor and pupil strikes. It meant co-operative grocery stores. It meant confronting political corruption head on and working to ensure fair elections. It meant holding business operators accountable for providing their employees with adequate wages and safe working conditions. It meant, according to one worker quoted in Perry's memoir, "rubbing heads with dedicated folk for the good of the poor and common people."

This is not to say that Perry's strategies are timeless or that they can be effortlessly applied forty years later. But if you're invested in arguing that Appalachians are trapped in the past—and especially if you make a name or living from it—it seems disingenuous to not find out what people in the past *actually did* to address poverty and inequality.

RADICAL HILLBILLIES

Here is another image, and perhaps its subjects will be more familiar. A young African American man, in short sleeves with his jacket draped over his arm, is grinning in front of a library. A similarly attired African American man, somewhat stouter, has his head turned toward two women, a young white girl who appears to be speaking to the group and an older African American woman in a long skirt and glasses. A white man with a broad smile is slightly behind them, a foot taller than anyone else in the frame. Posed but engrossed in conversation, only one subject is actually looking at the camera.

The smaller African American man is twenty-eight year old Martin Luther King, Jr., flanked by his friends Rosa Parks, Pete Seeger, and Ralph Abernathy. The young white girl is Charis Horton, the daughter of Myles Horton, co-founder of the Highlander Folk School, where the group assembled in 1957. The occasion was the twenty-fifth anniversary of the school, founded in 1932 in the coal-mining town of Monteagle, Tennessee. Two years later, the state would seize the school because a workshop attendee left twenty-five cents beside a drink cooler stocked with beer. The state, flexing its longstanding animosity toward the school for its opposition to segregation, argued that Highlander had violated its charter by selling liquor without an appropriate license.

"You can padlock a building," Horton said, as the state took his school, "but you can't padlock an idea." Another image comes into frame, a press photograph of a man laughing as the door to Horton's beloved school is chained.

Here is another image, more sinister and this time on a billboard. It's the same young Martin Luther King, Jr., at the Highlander Folk School. An arrow is pointing to him, emblazoned with text that reads "MARTIN LUTHER KING, JR. AT COMMUNIST TRAINING SCHOOL." The billboards began appearing in 1965, the year that King led a five-day march to Selma, Alabama. They used images created by Ed Friend, an investigator for the Georgia Commission on Education, which was operating at that time as an anti-integration watchdog group. Friend surreptitiously filmed and photographed the twenty-fifth anniversary celebrations at Highlander and helped turn the fruits of his labor into a widely distributed "educational pamphlet" that linked the school and its associates to the Communist Party.

Friend's films of the Highlander Folk School, used as anti-segregation propaganda, are unintentionally blissful. Children are everywhere and many are swimming in a lake that bordered Highlander's farm. People are dancing. There are no racial divisions, no divisions based on gender or age.

This, too, is Appalachia. Appalachia is images of strikes and strife and land hollowed out for coal, but it is also images of joy and freedom. Our album is filled with images of people who suffered, but also people who fought.

Highlander persists today. It still operates out of East Tennessee, now as the Highlander Research and Education Center. In September 2017 the organization will celebrate its eighty-fifth anniversary. Many of the platforms supported by the organization will be recognizable. #BlackLivesMatter, Fightfor15, and mobilization against the Dakota Access Pipeline all received recent support. In other words, the Highlander Research and Education Center still focuses on Appalachian issues because the fight for racial, environmental, and labor justice—wherever it takes place—is always our fight as well.

THEY SAY IN HARLAN COUNTY

The history of eastern Kentucky is special to me because the people of eastern Kentucky asked us a question that demanded, and still demands an answer: Which side are you on?

During the 1930s, at the height of the first war in Harlan County between miners and coal operators—and you should know enough of our history by now to understand there will be another—the second most dangerous occupation, after mining, was operating a grocery store. In eastern Kentucky, people were starving. Harlan-area coal operators cut wages during the Great Depression, precipitating a fierce battle between members of the United Mine Workers and the private armies commanded by coal operators, their numbers strengthened by the use of the National Guard as strikebreakers. Working people were homeless, evicted from company housing for their union sympathies, and store owners feared widespread looting.

Tillman Cadle, a striking miner, would often spend his mornings at his local A&P, hoping that store owners might distribute what provisions they could spare. He remembered looking through the store's windows with an awareness that his labor made possible everything that was in front of him. The lives and deaths of men like Cadle provided the fuel to process and transport food. As he stared into the store, he often thought, "We worked to make all that good food, yet there's a piece of glass between us." When I am asked who or what Appalachia is, I think of that piece of glass. I think of sides and boundaries and both the horror and solidarity of knowing one's place.

The store owners, incidentally, did provide provisions to striking miners, especially those with children. And for their generosity the commonwealth rewarded them with charges of "criminal syndicalism," the same language used to prosecute the Bradens in 1954 and the Mulloys and McSurelys in 1968.

When I think of the Harlan County in the 1970s, another coal war on repeat, I think of more glass, but this time it's the glass of a camera lens. I see Robert Gumpert's photographs, and Barbara Kopple's fierce documentary *Harlan County, U.S.A.* I see an elderly woman on a picket line, holding a sign that reads, "DUKE ENERGY OWNS THE BROOKSIDE MINE, BUT THEY DON'T OWN US." I see women in jail, women pulling guns from underneath their shirts. I see striking miners, milling around the mortal remains of a young man named Lawrence Jones—pieces of his brain left on the ground where a strikebreaker murdered him. I hear his fellow workers mourn, "That's the brains of a goddamned fellow who tried to do something."

If you saw through my eyes you'd see hands in pockets and hands on guns and toes on picket lines. You'd see an Appalachia made from funeral wreaths and breathing apparatuses, union banners and tapestries decorated with images of JFK. You'd see our parents and grandparents. You'd see men and women thinking of *their* parents and grandparents, who fought and died for the same damn things.

You'd see Florence Reece, singing out for us to answer which side we're on. You'd see Barbara Kopple running toward strikebreakers in defense of miners. You'd see how easy it is to become one of us like Kopple did. No need to write a sad book or platform yourself constantly, just run toward your friends when they need you. You'd see the exhaustion of waking up before sunrise every day to be shot or jailed. You'd see people buried alive to make energy, forced to splice electrical cables knee-deep in flooded mines. You'd see men who worked with one eye on the roof, one eye on the coal, and a mind full of dreams of anywhere fresh and green. You'd hear their complaints and the response from the coal company. Over and over, "Just get your bucket. Get your bucket. Get your bucket."

To cleanse my mind of violence, when I think of eastern Kentucky, I also think of Eula Hall. I see her in the 1980s, standing in the ashes of the health clinic she created, and that she would rebuild and fill with photographs. I try to imagine her as a fifteen-year-old girl from Greasy Creek, Kentucky, getting booted from a canning factory in New York during the Second World War for inciting a labor riot.

Hall opened the Mud Creek Health Clinic in 1973 out of a trailer in her yard. Like many Appalachians, she saw the War on Poverty pass the most desperate Appalachians by. Access to basic healthcare was, as it is today, a life or death issue in rural communities. With the help of volunteers, the clinic offered poor rural folk, many of whom suffered from health problems caused by their work in the mines, health services at little or no cost. When the Mud Creek Health Clinic outgrew the trailer, Hall moved operations into her home and lived in her yard.

Arsonists burned down the clinic in 1982 but it never ceased operations. Hall and her staff saw patients in the yard and she called the telephone company to ask for a telephone line in her tree. When it refused, she told them that if the telephone company could put a phone down a coal mine, it could come and put a phone in her damn tree. Hall got her phone line, and eventually, she was able to rebuild her clinic. The Mud Creek Health Clinic still operates out of Grethel, Kentucky, a place memorialized by *People* magazine as "so remote that if you press the scan button on a car radio, the numbers keep going round without finding a station."

UP THE RIDGE

I see images of Virginia too, images of caravans snaking up mountains to places where our hidden communities are kept. At dusk, car headlights from men on shift work illuminate the products of our most wretched talents: our ability to flatten mountains with astounding efficiency. What we installed in their place, however, are not mines. No, these images of dark and cold light are not of the earth and no one is marching up the mountain toward freedom. Quite the opposite.

The most profound example I can give you of how the past, present, and future collide in Appalachia is to tell you about the prison industry here, and about the individuals who fight it. After the mines closed, the prisons came. People desperate to replace their only source of employment opened their communities and tore apart the mountains to imprison people deemed the most violent and dangerous offenders. Like in times past, local people saw the degradation of human dignity and the exploitation of labor and land and fought against it using familiar methods.

In the prison industrial complex, inmates are commodities. They are bought and sold and transferred according to the cost of beds and the cost of land and the cost of the labor required to imprison them. In the 1990s, two prison systems opened in southwest Virginia. Their construction offered state and federal prison officials a captive and compliant workforce contained in a location that would torment inmates with bleak and alien geography. Most inmates, of course, would be African American, arriving from the Northeast or lowland South. Central Appalachia would soon become one of the most concentrated areas of prison growth in the country.

The arrival of Wallens Ridge State Prison and its sister institution, Red Onion State Prison, worried area community groups and media organizations in southwest Virginia and eastern Kentucky. Residents began to see that the communities of prisoners and their families were also now part of their lives.

Community media organization Appalshop, based in Whitesburg, Kentucky, and radio affiliate WMMT became hubs not just for news and communication about the prisons, but places where incarcerated men and their families, separated by hundreds of miles, tried to connect with one another. WMMT's radio signal reached the prisons, and staff began to receive letters from the new prisoners describing loneliness and abusive conditions.

Media artists Nick Szuberla and Amelia Kirby began a radio show for prisoners that played hip-hop music and brought news from the places they called home. Szuberla remembered that, "The [prison] community came to us in the form of letters, clearly describing human rights violations and racism within our newly built prisons." In response to this need—to acknowledge the presence of the incarcerated in their communities—Szuberla and Kirby began to connect to the families of prisoners, who sometimes called or wrote their show. This quickly became the primary focus of their slot, to pass on messages by encouraging family members to call into the show and speak to their loved ones via radio.

The two artists also created a documentary about the prisons produced by Appalshop, 2006's *Up the Ridge*, which examines the prison industrial complex in a local, national, and global context. Occasionally, locals who kept the prison's problems at a distance experienced a change of heart listening to their show. Others transformed the stories of prisoners into community theater productions with the help of prison abolition groups and with permission from the families.

In 2010, WMMT DJ Sylvia Ryerson joined the decade-old radio program—re-branded as "Calls from Home"—which by then had a national audience thanks to the internet. Ryerson expanded the program and began to organize transportation for the prisoners' families to visit their loved ones. Raymond Thompson, a photographer from West Virginia University, documented these journeys for his *Justice Undone* project. Both Thompson and Ryerson's work was highlighted in 2016 by the Marshall Project. Ryerson now does long-form radio postcards she calls "Restorative Radio," created for specific individuals that allow them to sonically travel to, for example, their children's birthday parties. "Rather than documenting the barriers to staying connected," she writes, "each audio postcard enacts meaningful communication in spite of such barriers."

In 2015, Congress set aside over four hundred million dollars for the construction of a new correctional facility in Letcher County, Kentucky. "You are Letcher County, Kentucky. You are rural, mountainous, and in the heart of the central Appalachian coalfields. Your economy is not in good shape. Fox News has called your town 'the poster child for the war on coal.' You are offered funds to build a new federal prison. It could bring jobs but also brings up troubling moral issues. What do you do?" asked Benny Becker from WMMT.

Letcher County congressional representative Hal Rogers, the former Chair of the House Appropriations Committee, believes the prison will transform the area's economy. But there are fifteen prisons within a one-hundred-mile radius and local economies have not been transformed. Local labor fills the lowest paid positions, offering starting salaries of just $16,000 to $24,000 a year. Transferred employees with seniority take the better compensated roles, but in anticipation of their next transfer, they are reluctant to purchase homes or put down roots in the community. In some rural prison communities, only 10 to 20 percent of the workers, who all have to pass stringent background and credit checks, are local. Most of the counties that house prisons remain among the poorest parts of the state.

Examining prison construction only as a failed method of rural economic development, however, slights the moral repugnance of the prison industrial complex, which many rightly call a tool of the new Jim Crow. For activists in Central Appalachia, the racism of the prison industrial complex is central to their political and community organizing. Tarence Ray, an organizer with the Letcher County Governance Project, a community group that formed to oppose the proposed prison, believes that bringing prisons to rural, predominately white communities fits an established pattern of pitting poor white individuals against African American people by convincing them that their economic survival depends on supporting structures that harm and oppress.

The Letcher County Governance Project held a silent protest during Hal Roger's presentation at the most recent Shaping Our Appalachian Region economic conference. The fate of the prison is currently in limbo; the draft of Trump's first budget eliminated its funding. Kentucky politicians, however, are confident that congressional action to save the prison will prevail.

Appalachian prison abolition is, in many ways, a perfect storm of new regional activism. The movement is led by young people who connect the legacy of anti-coal and anti-poverty activists to modern causes. They are often anti-capitalists, a tradition that has a long history in Appalachia. As the work of Appalshop and WMMT demonstrates, community organizers are skillful storytellers and communicators committed to the idea that telling our stories is central to our activism. And they see, as the most passionate among us do, that our communities are connected. Wallens Ridge is a prison in southwestern Virginia, but it is also a telephone number on speed dial at the home of loved ones in Connecticut, and a place that absorbs a radio signal from eastern Kentucky.

YESTERDAY'S PEOPLE

"Appalachian programs can succeed only if they are based on an understanding of the mountaineer's personality and the need to preserve his identity, according to *Yesterday's People: Life in Contemporary Appalachia* by Jack E. Weller…In the simplest form and the plainest language possible, he has created an indispensable handbook for anyone who really hopes to understand and ultimately help these charter members of the Other America," reads the brittle book review, clipped and cut from an ancient newspaper. Its usual duty is to act as a bookmark in my partner's copy of *Yesterday's People*, but I disturbed its slumber not long ago to scan and send it to a particularly defensive fan of *Hillbilly Elegy*.

For a number of reasons, Weller's 1965 handbook doesn't rub me the wrong way as other cultural or sociological studies of the region do, although it proceeds using much the same "strange and peculiar people" logic, which you may have deduced from the title. The chief reason is that Weller, originally from New York, inadvertently makes Appalachian people sound fantastic at times.

Weller's purpose, in essence, is to explain Appalachians' differences from middle-class Americans *to* a middle-class American audience. He writes descriptions like, "the mountaineer has found his way of life satisfying enough, and he looks on people of other classes without a trace of envy or jealousy…the mountaineer rejects the status-seeking, social climbing, 'get rich,' let's-have-fun orientation, which he pictures as the middle class."

Another favorite passage: "Though the mountain man often pays little attention to the larger children, he will make a great deal of fuss over babies, fondling them, and carrying them about…I have seen teenage boys take a crying infant from its mother's arms during church, amusing it for the rest of the service with an interest and tenderness which is almost unbelievable."

The other reason I regard Weller with a kinder eye is that I once heard a story about the end of his life. When he was dying, suffering from Alzheimer's, he asked to be taken to the mountains one last time. According to the story, in moments when his fog lifted, he spoke of his regret for *Yesterday's People*. To carry his burdens to the mountains and speak his regret is perhaps one of the most Appalachian things a person can do. I accept Weller not for what he did, but for what he became at the end, which is one of us. This story might well be bogus but I offer Weller as proof that I do not hold earth-shattering grudges toward everyone who's ever authored a problematic study of Appalachia.

But I am also citing *Yesterday's People* for another reason. While Weller was compiling his handbook about the region's "primitive" people, those very same people were engaged in business of their own. They were not looking for saviors but instead set to work consolidating their collective power to create political change for the good of their communities.

The initial scenes of the 1969 documentary *Before the Mountain Was Moved* are excruciating. As poor West Virginians repair cemeteries and dig out cars destroyed by strip mining, they explain the meaning of life in Appalachia. "He just laughed at me," one woman said, explaining her conversation with a strip mine operator about damage his equipment caused to her home, "He said it was an act of God."

Despite this healthy appreciation for the work of the almighty, a following scene shows coal operators assaulting elderly men and women as they attempt to enter their church. In the midst of an overwhelming threat of violence and retaliation, the community decides that night to travel to Charleston to express their concerns about strip mining and to ask for corrective legislation from state lawmakers. This becomes the momentum that drives *Before the Mountain Was Moved*; the personal and collective journeys taken by ordinary men and women to stop the destruction of their community.

One of the most interesting moments in the documentary is when community residents use a long car trip to discuss what we would today call white privilege. Led by an African American woman, the riders remember moments when white members of the community benefitted from their whiteness, and moments when they experienced collective oppression with their Black neighbors. It is not a "kumbaya" scene by any means—the white passengers are uncomfortable but yield the conversation to their African American neighbor—but it is something we are told never happens in Appalachia. There is no interracial solidarity or even conflict in Appalachia because people of color rarely exist in the worlds popular authors create for us.

The community *does* win its anti-strip-mining legislation. The scene where they learn of their victory is warm and wonderful. We find them on a rainy evening, peering out the windows to the mountains above, anxious about the boulders that might be washed down below. But then comes the breaking news that state lawmakers have supported their legislation by a margin of ninety-eight to one. Suddenly anxiety becomes relief. There is dancing and singing, and in the middle of the celebration, an elderly man who has been used by the coal industry his entire life shouts, "They've heard the voice of the people!" We want this moment to last forever for them because we know what's coming will be worse.

MOUNTAINTOP REMOVAL AND
THE NEVER-ENDING BATTLE OF BLAIR MOUNTAIN

Few places symbolize the currents of Appalachian history like Blair Mountain. After the labor uprising there in 1921, the mountain became a direct link to the region's radical history. It's also a handy piece of evidence to counter people who tell you that your heritage is one of complacency. But while the people of Appalachia might own the memory of Blair Mountain, coal companies still own much of the land.

Mountaintop removal—the practice of blowing the top of a mountain off to make extraction easier and cheaper for coal companies—renders both mountains and miners into abstract and disposable commodities, which is part of its design. It is no coincidence that the rate of mountaintop removal rose in tandem with increased hostility to organized labor in West Virginia in the 1980s.

Mountaintop removal requires fewer workers. Coal companies have further increased economic instability by using subcontracted labor instead of permanent employees, another common union-busting strategy. It is understandable that, for some miners, working on the surface of a mountain is preferable to working underground. But it is also true that mountaintop removal has intensified environmental destruction while surrounding communities have become poorer as stable jobs have dwindled.

Mountaintop removal and parallel narratives about the "war on coal" divide communities, which also benefits the coal industry. In *Matewan*, the romanticized but powerful film about the prelude to the Battle of Blair Mountain, a union organizer tells an assembled crowd, "There ain't but two sides, them that work and them that don't." What was once a framework of solidarity has, in parts of coal country, become a distorted way of assigning authority to a limited number of people who are allowed to speak about the coal industry. To question the logic of the industry is, in essence, to question the logic of your neighbor having a job or your cousin having health insurance. The coal industry endows us with messy identities—the "I'm not a coal miner, but…" qualification—designed to maximize conflict.

It's difficult to overstate the degree to which mountaintop removal has changed life and work in parts of Appalachia. It is clear that Donald Trump conceals his love of coal as a commodity in his over-performed and insincere admiration for coal miners. He is not original in this strategy. He borrowed it directly from the coal industry. People outside the region, and particularly mainstream media, take great joy in pointing out these contradictions as if only they can see them, lobbing rhetorical questions to an imagined audience of coal miners: "Why have you voted against your own interests?" This question only seems relevant if you believe that individuals who were convinced to dismantle mountains can't also be convinced to vote for outcomes beneficial to their employers.

Into this mix came in 2009 the second Battle for Blair Mountain, a multifront campaign to protect the land from mountaintop removal and to recognize its cultural and historical significance to West Virginia. And once again, West Virginia's coal companies reacted with their peculiar brand of hysteria to what they perceived to be an assault on their fundamental right to own not only the land and its resources, but also the region's history.

In the winter of 2009, the Department of the Interior (DOI) accepted an application to place Blair Mountain on the National Register of Historic Places. Placement of a site on the register is often more symbolic than strategic, but sometimes it is both. The register guarantees no federal protections, but it does obligate parties to make a good-faith attempt to limit damage to sites of cultural and historical significance. In the case of Blair Mountain it might mean, for example, that companies owning coal leases at the site would be obligated to forgo extraction via mountaintop removal in favor of less efficient subterranean mining methods.

There's a particular form of coal industry math in which jobs that have never existed are perpetually taken away. In Logan and Mingo Counties, coal companies claimed that efforts to protect the mountain's cultural heritage were stealing jobs from surrounding communities, despite the fact that subterranean extraction would require more workers. Deep resentment developed in coal country, this time not between miners and coal operators, but between conservationists and the industry at large, including non-union miners.

The application remained on the register for six months until the DOI de-listed it in response to claims of "procedural errors" made by the West Virginia state historic preservation office. This is the point where the story turns into a shit show of the highest order, even for coal country. On one side of the table were the coal companies, their legal teams, and the state's preservation office, who argued that the original application failed to solicit comments from individuals with an important legal interest in Blair Mountain. And on the other side were archaeologists, historians, conservationists, and their legal representative who offered the very straightforward response that there was no conflict because a bit more investigation would have easily revealed those parties were long dead.

As organizations instigated lawsuits to see the mountain returned to the register, activist groups in Appalachia took a more direct approach. They decided, once again, to march on Blair Mountain and reclaim their history from the coal industry. The 2011 march included individuals from sixty-five organizations, supported by celebrities and politicians. Jason Bostic, the vice president of the West Virginia Coal Association, summed up the coal industry's response when he looked out on a snaking line of 1,500 people marching up a mountain in ninety-degree weather and asked, "What good is a mountain just to have a mountain?" The second Battle of Blair Mountain foregrounded ecological conservation, but it was about labor as well. The United Mine Workers of America helped sponsor the march, concerned about their history and the ongoing erosion of workers' rights in southern West Virginia.

"Behold the road to Blair Mountain, where another civil war looms in the hills of Appalachia," Chuck Keeney wrote, describing the community divisions opened by the march. Watching footage captured by marchers is a deeply uncomfortable experience. A pickup crawls by with a homemade banner that reads, "FUCK YOU TREEHUGGERS." It's followed by another truck and another banner, this time, "FUCK YOU SONS OF BITCHES I LOVE COAL." Children scream at marchers and ask them, mimicking their parents, "Have you ever worked a day in your life?"

The wives of coal truck operators, who believe their husbands will be fired if the protest delays their deliveries, are filmed telling bewildered West Virginians to "go back where you came from." Marchers attempt to move a boulder intentionally rolled onto the road from a mining site and young men jeer at them. One tells the group of activists that the 1921 miners would be ashamed of them because they had taken up arms for their right to mine coal. "They fought to unionize. Do you work at a unionized mine?" an organizer corrects him, to a blank stare. A mind remained unchanged but a boulder got moved.

Good news for Blair Mountain came in 2014 when a court of appeals ruled that petitioners—who by that point included the Sierra Club, Friends of Blair Mountain, the Ohio Valley Environmental Coalition, the West Virginia Labor History Association, and the National Trust for Historic Preservation—

could move forward with a legal challenge to vacate the DOI's de-listing of the site. In 2016, a federal judge ruled that the DOI had violated federal law, and a second agreed that the agency had acted in an "arbitrary and capricious" manner by rubber-stamping the state's evidence using a process that contained "very little, if any, indicia of reasoned decision making."

Despite this procedural victory, Blair Mountain remains in limbo. It has not yet been returned to the National Register. It may never get there. It exists in the space between the question, "What good is a mountain just to have a mountain?" and Judy Bonds's assertion that "there are no jobs on a dead planet." In that regard, the Battle of Blair Mountain is never-ending, looped, and waiting for its next generation of soldiers.

GETTING APPALACHIA LESS WRONG

There once existed in the field of Appalachian Studies a model of Appalachia as an "internal colony." Looking at this framework— what it did and didn't do—is a good way of considering how we all, Appalachians included, might be able to get Appalachia a little less wrong.

After the War on Poverty failed, many Appalachians came to believe that the region's problems could not be fixed without the help of local experts, whose coherent sense of history could drive social change. The War on Poverty had attempted to address Appalachia's problems in a top-down fashion, anchored in the belief that change could take place within the region's existing economic, social, and political structures. When this strategy proved to be inadequate, Appalachians set out to define the region's problems in their own language and according to their own experiences.

The "internal colony" model came courtesy of 1978's *Colonialism in Modern America: The Appalachian Case,* by Helen Lewis, Linda Johnson, and Donald Askins. It defined the region's long history of destruction in the name of capitalism as a form of colonialism. It also understood the use of stereotypes and myths as an extension of colonization. The "internal colony" model gave many Appalachians, for the first time, a tool for understanding the region's web of exploitation, from the stories of local color writers in the early nineteenth century to the corruption that fueled the domination of the coal industry in the twentieth.

Scholar Mary K. Anglin reflected on the work as "an activist interpretation grounded in a sense of place and a reading of social hierarchy, principally through the lens of class relations." It is not surprising that individuals living in a region considered a "third world" by Americans might believe theories of colonialism spoke to their experiences as well. The theory, quite accurately, presented unchecked capitalism as the root of Appalachia's problems. Following the priorities of the radical Left, it also called for an anti-colonial movement in Appalachia.

The "internal colony" model is deeply satisfying but problematic. Students of Appalachia such as myself experienced powerful epiphanies examining this model, which allowed us to transform our shame into coherent and righteous anger. Ada Smith, a founder of the Stay Together Appalachia Youth Project, said that the model "allowed me to understand that my people, my heritage, and culture were not the problem, and gave me a way in which I could more easily understand power…This in turn connected me to issues around racism, classism, and homophobia because of their structural nature."

Barbara Smith and Steve Fisher wrote that the emotional power of the "internal colony" model helped students of Appalachia better situate the logic of "place-based exploitation…with cultural degradation" and work against it. "It thereby *creates* Appalachia as a regional collectivity, no longer pathologized but oppressed, and enables us to situate ourselves in a shared cultural geography that recognizes all residents as heirs to a special, place-based identity," which in turn "draws an undeniably powerful line between innocent victims inside the region and profiteering elites on the outside."

The model appeared at a time when there was intense interest in the region to determine who exactly "owned" Appalachia. In 1977, widespread flooding in Kentucky and West Virginia, exacerbated by mining activity, left hundreds homeless. When relief agencies tried to construct temporary housing for victims, they could find no suitable combination of land that was both dry and not controlled by obstructive corporate entities. The following year, the Appalachian Regional Commission and the Appalachian Alliance launched the Appalachian Land Study, which used participatory action research to document and map patterns of land ownership in the region.

Their findings, released in 1981, confirmed what most had long suspected: that outside corporations owned the majority of the region's mineral rights and almost half its surface land. The study also found that the property taxes of non-corporate land owners were offsetting the taxes on land owned by corporations. In one county, for example, corporations that owned 70 percent of the land contributed just 4 percent of the county's property tax stream. Not surprisingly, communities where such a stark imbalance existed experienced sharp declines in quality of life.

The "internal colony" model, therefore, reflected what was true in 1978 and is still true today; that the region's uneven distribution of wealth and resources is a significant obstacle in efforts to address Appalachian poverty. This portal, however, also reflected imbalances of its own. The use of a colony model to understand modern Appalachia elides the region's history of indigenous colonization and the continued marginalization of Native American individuals both within Appalachia and the wider United States. As Emily Satterwhite wrote, "The idea of Appalachia as racially distinct, rural, and premodern has served to reassure white Americans of the persistence of an indigenous white national culture."

In rare moments when intellectuals praise Appalachia, and more often in moments when we praise ourselves, even those of us who are white are endowed with indigenous cultural traits. We are keepers and stewards of the land, for example, fighting the encroachment of destructive forces. For some, this cultural identity fosters solidarity between indigenous and non-indigenous people in Appalachia. There is and was, for example, enormous support among Appalachian activist groups for indigenous water-protectors at Standing Rock. At the same time, native land rights continue to be an afterthought in more contemporary discussions of corporate land ownership, one of many tensions that must be interrogated and reconciled in post-coal strategic visioning.

The "internal colony" model also situates the problems of Appalachia as imported woes inflicted on the region by a revolving cast of outsiders. It risks excusing us from the responsibility of imagining how we in the region might be complicit in structural inequality and oppression. A chief example of this is the support for the coal industry found among Appalachia's political elite, but equally important are the homophobia, racism, and xenophobia within the region. Appalachian author Silas House writes, "Homophobia lurks in the hollers and slithers along the ridges in Appalachia. The reason why is because Appalachia is in America. What is happening here is happening throughout the rest of the country."

In Appalachia, there's a tendency to believe that tensions only occur when outsiders meddle in our business. This is a benevolent stereotype that stretches back more than 150 years. Anthropologist Allen Batteau called it the myth of "Holy Appalachia"—a fiction designed to help repair a society contaminated by the evils of slavery. During and after the Civil War, it became therapeutic, in a sense, to allow a category of white persons to be immune from racial hysteria. In other words, white Appalachians became the first beneficiaries of #notallwhitepeople.

Citing the existence of Appalachian anti-slavery societies and our geographic and cultural distance from plantation slavery, intellectuals from Abraham Lincoln to Carter G. Woodson have made the case for our racial innocence. If the institution of slavery fundamentally altered the moral compass of white individuals, it followed that those who lacked exposure to it could be spared. White people in Appalachia used this myth of racial innocence frequently for many years, most visibly of late in Vance's popular claims that white Trump voters in Appalachia are a different breed, uncontaminated by racism.

The myth of "Holy Appalachia" returned to use when white supremacists converged on Pikeville, Kentucky, at the end of April 2017. Organized by the Traditionalist Worker Party, members of the League of the South, the Oath Keepers, and the Nationalist Social Party rallied in Pikeville in "defense of white families." White supremacists have often tried to gain a foothold in Appalachia and center the region in projected fantasies that combine white racial solidarity with economic uplift. In response to the rally, militant leftists, anti-racists, and anti-fascists planned a counter-protest. The city of Pikeville passed special ordinances explicitly intended to discourage counter-protest, many businesses in the area closed for the duration of the rally, and locals with the ability to leave for the weekend were encouraged to do so.

Local commentary about the rally from both regional media and residents emphasized that Pikeville had done nothing to encourage the rally. The commentary took pains to suggest that both the white supremacist demonstrators and counter-protestors were all outsiders. News reports made it a point of sharing, as an editor from *TriState Update* did, that "many of the cars TWP members left in had out-of-state license plates. Some were from California, Alabama, and Georgia just to name a few."

Writing for the *Huffington Post*, Kentucky native Jason Belcher wrote that "local citizens did not turn out to support any of the groups…Conservative Republicans and liberal Democrats here don't agree on much, but we agree extremism has no place in Pikeville." Dave Mistich, of the *100 Days in Appalachia* project, framed the event as the "white supremacist rally and counter protest that no one wanted here." Mistich wrote, "Participants from both sides were mostly from out of state, leaving locals few and far between Saturday afternoon in downtown Pikeville." According to these local voices, Pikeville is a place of folksy neutrality where the good and the bad cancel each other out as long as no one steps out of line and becomes "an extremist."

Pikeville, you may remember, is the same place where the wealthy and powerful tormented community activists and charged organizers with sedition. Eastern Kentucky, you also may remember, is immortalized in one of the most recognizable anthems of the labor and civil rights movements as a place where there is no neutrality. There are many things that have come to Appalachia that no one wanted, but how we respond to them once they're here is important.

Many local residents did indeed counter-protest; their willingness to do so was a product of life in communities shaped by racism. They marched, some wearing red bandanas, and captured video of the event that they later set to bluegrass music and shared in forums populated by other Appalachians. One protester explained, "Well, Nazis put out a call to white families to come here, and I'm here as the mother of a white family to say that Nazis aren't welcome in Appalachia. We have real problems here with pipelines, oil and gas and coal companies are poisoning water and air. A few people are getting rich while our children get sick and Nazis come in and tell us to blame that on other poor people because they have a different color skin? Please."

Local counter-protestors took explicit steps to connect their identities as both Appalachians and anti-racists and put this identity to work in the service of social change. It's a form of activism that, much like the racism that compelled them to act, is wholly consistent with the region's history.

You'll often hear, in the region, variations on the belief that "hillbillies are the only group it's still socially acceptable to belittle." This is not the case, not by a long shot. What is true, however, is that people are often blindly classist while remaining self-congratulatory about their other progressive credentials.

One of the most insidious manifestations of this attitude is the belief that people could escape the problems of the region if they would just move. This attitude rarely acknowledges the personal factors that may impact someone's desire to move. Rather, it flatly equates migration with opportunity in ways that are disappointing. The *National Review* is fond of preaching, for example, variations on Kevin Williamson's painful but popular advice that poor people "need real opportunity, which means they need real change, which means they need U-Hauls." Let me tell you how that worked out for me.

JUST MOVE

Appalachians are a group of people burdened with the task of perpetually re-earning our place in narratives of American progress. In this we are not alone. For us, however, this burden manifests in calls for migration and the de-population of our home, an exodus of sacrifice that must be performed in order to prove that we are not the people you think we are. To leave is to demonstrate our ambition, to be something other than dependent and stubborn. To leave is to be productive rather than complacent, and to refuse is to be complicit. Theories of "brain drain" suggest that the only individuals willing to be left behind are those who are pathological, choosing to forgo a chance at prosperity to live among the lost.

I left. I earned a PhD and promptly moved where the job market sent me, which happened to be southeast Texas. The move was wholly in line with notions of appropriate mobility, particularly for those with an elite education who take their place in a system of privilege that narrows as it elevates. In other words, I am a product of two worlds that demand a particular path of ambition: the mountains and the academy. The logic of the academy reinforced that I should accept any position, no matter how remote the location or how awful the pay, to be successful.

The corner of Tennessee I come from is not known for its coal extraction, but it is known for transforming that coal into energy through the all-encompassing hand of the Tennessee Valley Authority. Its power-generating facilities produce coal-ash, a particularly toxic substance that defies convenient disposal. Using the TVA's own data, the Southern Environmental Law Center estimates that over the last sixty years, twenty-seven billion gallons of coal-ash have leaked from the utility company's Gallatin facility, one of six such plants in Tennessee.

Steve Hale and Steve Cavendish, writing for the *Nashville Scene*, described a 2008 industrial spill not far from me, "Around 1 a.m., the retaining wall of an 80 acre ash pond at the Kingston Fossil Plant 40 miles from Knoxville collapsed, sending 50 years of waste spilling out into the night. In all, 1.1 billion gallons of wet ash rushed forth from the plant—a tidal wave of toxic sludge that covered some 300 acres, spilled into a nearby river and destroyed three homes, sweeping at least one off its foundation." The TVA responded by purchasing 180 contaminated properties and 960 toxic acres of land. Five years after the spill, only Tommy Charles and his wife were left in his neighborhood. He cried when reporters came to ask him why he didn't leave. At the age of seventy-four, he didn't have anywhere else to go.

If the logic of exodus was correct, then my relocation would forever entitle me to be spared the sight of people weeping for their homes. It would exempt me from conversations with bank tellers about the worsening symptoms of their children's asthma. My daily commute would be forever free from the monotonous rush to roll up windows at certain mile markers. My water would be drinkable and my air clean. I would be paid my worth, allowed to live in productive comfort among others allowed the same.

This is not the reality I experienced. Instead, I followed the market to the polluted air and contaminated water of Texas's "cancer belt," this time brought to you by the oil industry. Here, the poor people most likely to suffer the worst effects of refinery pollution are African American, not white, but the same brutal disregard is present. But this time it was me weeping for my home—both the one I left and the one I came to.

When I traveled to give academic talks or to interview for other positions, I became convinced that the smell of refineries followed me, on my clothes, and would reveal my true identity: someone not important enough to not be poisoned. The logic of exodus just shrugs its shoulders at these realities and tells us to move smarter. I decided to ignore this logic and come back home to fight smarter.

The relief at returning is overwhelming, to come creeping again toward home. Silas House writes, "There is a language in the kudzu and it is all ours and belongs to no one else. This is my tongue for you, whispering our history: words words words."

CONCLUSION

In 2012, community organizer Si Kahn shared a story at a conference in Pennsylvania about union activist Florence Reece. Reece wrote one of the labor movement's most powerful anthems—"Which Side Are You On?"—about the harassment of her family by anti-union thugs in eastern Kentucky in the 1930s. Kahn retold a conversation he had with Reece much later in her life about the day she wrote her song.

According to legend, Reece became so angry that she tore a calendar off the wall, letting the words flow onto its pages. "I could never understand," Kahn said, "how Florence Reece could write down five whole verses on one of those calendars" crammed with information like "phases of the moon the moon didn't even know it had. There's just no room to do that."

"Si," the voice of the now-departed Reece patiently answered in the story, "before I started writing I turned it over."

"We need to make a deceptively simple decision," Kahn concluded, "No one has ever laid it out more clearly than Florence Reece…Part of our work now and for the next fifty years is to turn everything over."

And then the people sang, in voices bright and loud, the song that Reece gave us.

Fifty years is not just an arbitrary dateline in Appalachia. We gather in these spaces of collective dreaming to sing and bear witness with the hope that we might call into being the end of what Rebecca Scott called "the dismal banality of the dominion of coal." In Appalachia, coal isn't just coal. It's the blackest part of a constellation of knowledge that tells us it is easier in our world to bury a person alive than lift her up.

"Mountaintop removal is an act of radical violence," says the People's Pastoral, our theology of liberation popular among some Catholics in the mountains, "that leaves monstrous scars across Earth's body resembling moonscapes, dead zones on our planet which cannot be restored to their prior life-giving condition. Many people who see these wounds close up lament: 'This is what the end of the world looks like to me.'"

Ours is a region that makes graveyards for mountains, because companies have made our mountains into graveyards. "In his hands are the deep places of the Earth; the strength of the hills is His also," one gravestone reads, quoting Psalms.

There are, of course, individuals in the region who think the future of Appalachia is still coal black. But I prefer to think that it might be brighter, like the highlighter-colored shirts Larry Gibson wore, printed with his telephone number, daring us to care and reach out. Gibson died on the mountain he fought so hard to protect from mountaintop removal. In vain, rescuers transported him to a hospital where his daughter said, "You could smell the freshness of the air that was still on him. The dirt was embedded in his fingernails. It traced through every finger, every knuckle and every crease." Or it might be the bright purple of ironweed that Judy Bond pointed out to visiting reporters after her love for another ruined mountain earned her the Goldman Prize for environmental activism. "They say they're a symbol of Appalachian women," she said, "They're pretty. And their roots run deep. It's hard to move them."

In the early years of my training as a historian, I came across a photograph taken in Haysi, Virginia, in the 1930s, captured by a New Deal photographer. My grandfather's family is from Haysi and I became obsessed with this image and its mysterious origins because it profoundly challenged what I thought it meant to be Appalachian.

The image shows the interior of a tidy café with perfectly laid out checkered tablecloths. The time of day is ambiguous, but it is likely daytime—there is a backlight in the window that trained eyes can see. In the corner of the café is what appears to be a futuristic machine—an automatic photobooth. A well-dressed couple, their faces glowing from the camera's artificial light, sits inside. Leaning against the window is a young woman, waiting on her turn or waiting for her companions to be photographed. No one is paying attention to the photographer behind the government's camera.

My imagination ran wild when I looked at this image. Who brought a photobooth to Haysi, Virginia, a place populated by poor coal mining families? How long did it remain? Did anyone in my family use it? I ordered books on antique camera equipment from the library and imagined future plans to march into the National Archives in Washington, DC, my credentials as a historian in hand, and ask to see the image in person.

When the rush of questions abated, I realized that this was the first time I had looked closely at an image of Appalachia that didn't inspire shame or pain. I wasn't looking at the usual images of people trapped in poverty, intended to evoke pity. I was looking at a photograph of men and women apparently content, more interested in making their own images than the image being made of them. Because I viewed this image without feeling shame and pain, I could imagine myself in the future, a person who belonged in a cultural institution demanding to see my history.

Whatever happens next for Appalachia, there are people here who deserve similar moments of liberation from their pain and shame, to see their lives and history as something other than an incoherent parade of destruction and wretchedness. I hope that people in the region who keep fighting will, like the figures in my favorite photograph, turn away from anonymous cameras and capture their own images.

SUGGESTED RESOURCES

FICTION & POETRY

Andrews, Tom. *The Hemophiliac's Motorcycle*. Iowa City: University of Iowa Press, 1994.

Awiakta, Marilou. *Abiding Appalachia: Where Mountain and Atom Meet*. Memphis: St. Luke's Press, 1978.

Berry, Wendell. *The Country of Marriage*. Berkeley: Counterpoint Press, 1973.

Giardina, Denise. *Storming Heaven*. New York: Norton, 1987.

Gipe, Robert. *Trampoline: An Illustrated Novel*. Athens: Ohio University Press, 2015.

Giovanni, Nikki. *Cotton Candy on a Rainy Day*. New York: Harper Perennial, 1980.

Good, Crystal. *Valley Girl*. CreateSpace, 2012.

Haun, Mildred. *The Hawk's Done Gone*. Nashville: McNaughton & Gun, 1968.

Holbrook, Chris. *Upheaval*. Lexington: University Press of Kentucky, 2010.

House, Silas. *Clay's Quilt*. New York: Algonquin Books, 2001.

Howell, Rebecca Gayle. *Render*. Cleveland: Cleveland State University Poetry Center, 2013.

Manning, Maurice. *One Man's Dark*. Port Townsend, WA: Copper Canyon Press, 2017.

McKinney, Irene. *The Six O'Clock Mine Report.* Pittsburgh: University of Pittsburgh Press, 1989.

Miller, Jim Wayne. *The Brier Poems.* New York: Gnomon Press, 1997.

Norman, Gurney. *Kinfolks: The Wilgus Stories.* New York: Gnomon Press, 1977.

Offutt, Chris. *Kentucky Straight.* New York: Vintage Books, 1992.

Pancake, Ann. *Strange as This Weather Has Been.* Berkeley: Shoemaker & Hoard, 2007.

Pancake, Breece D'J. *The Stories of Breece D'J Pancake.* New York: Back Bay Books, 2002.

pluck! The Affrilachian Journal of Arts and Culture.

Rabble Lit–Working Class Literature.

Rash, Ron. *The World Made Straight.* New York: Henry Holt and Company, 2006.

Still, James. *River of Earth.* Lexington: University Press of Kentucky, 2014.

Taylor, Glenn. *A Hanging at Cinder Bottom: A Novel.* Portland: Tin House Books, 2015.

Walker, Frank X. *Affrilachia: Poems by Frank X Walker.* Lexington: Old Cove Press, 2000.

White, Charles Dodd and Larry Smith, eds. *Appalachia Now.* Huron, OH: Dog Bottom Press, 2015.

Wilkinson, Crystal. *The Birds of Opulence.* Lexington: University Press of Kentucky, 2016.

NON-FICTION

Bageant, Joe. *Deer Hunting with Jesus: Dispatches from America's Class War*. New York: Broadway Books, 2008.

Blizzard, William C. and Wess Harris. *When Miners March*. Oakland: PM Press, 2010.

DeRosier, Linda Scott. *Creeker: A Woman's Journey*. Lexington: University Press of Kentucky, 2002.

hooks, bell. *Belonging: A Culture of Place*. New York: Routledge, 2009.

Perry, Huey. *They'll Cut Off Your Project: A Mingo County Chronicle*. Morgantown: West Virginia University Press, 2011.

Mann, Jeff. *Loving Mountains, Loving Men*. Athens: University of Ohio Press, 2005.

McClanahan, Scott. *Crapalachia: A Biography of Place*. New York: Two Dollar Radio, 2013.

O'Brien, John. *At Home in the Heart of Appalachia*. New York: Anchor, 2002.

Offutt, Chris. *My Father the Pornographer*. New York: Washington Square Press, 2017.

Sonnie, Amy and James Tracy. *Hillbilly Nationalists, Urban Race Rebels, and Black Power*. New York: Melville House, 2011.

Tate, Linda. *Power in the Blood: A Family Narrative*. Athens: University of Ohio Press, 2009.

Thrash, Maggie. *Honor Girl: A Graphic Memoir*. Somerville, MA: Candlewick Press, 2015.

Trotter, Otis. *Keeping Heart: A Memoir of Family Struggle, Race, and Medicine*. Athens: Ohio University Press, 2015.

Verghese, Abraham. *My Own Country: A Doctor's Story of a Town and Its People in the Age of AIDS*. New York: Vintage Books, 1995.

Walls, Jeanette. *The Glass Castle*. New York: Scribner, 2006.

West Virginia Writers' Project. *West Virginia: A Guide to the Mountain State*. New York: Oxford University Press, 1941.

ACADEMIC HISTORY

Barkley, Frederick A. *Working Class Radicals: The Socialist Party in West Virginia, 1898-1920*. Morgantown: West Virginia University Press, 2012.

Billings, Dwight B. and Kathleen M. Blee. *The Road to Poverty: The Making of Wealth and Hardship in Appalachia*. New York: Cambridge University Press, 2000.

Billings, Dwight B., Gurney Norman and Katherine Ledford, eds. *Backtalk from Appalachia: Confronting Stereotypes*. Lexington, University Press of Kentucky, 2002.

Carney, Virginia Moore. *Eastern Band Cherokee Women: Cultural Persistence in their Letters and Speeches*. Knoxville: University of Tennessee Press, 2005.

Cook, Samuel R. *Monacans and Miners: Native American and Coal Mining Communities in Appalachia*. Lincoln: University of Nebraska Press, 2000.

Dunaway, Wilma A. *The First American Frontier: Transformation to Capitalism in Southern Appalachia, 1700-1860.* Chapel Hill: University of North Carolina Press, 1996.

Eller, Ronald D. *Miners, Millhands, and Mountaineers: Industrialization of the Appalachian South, 1880-1930.* Knoxville: University of Tennessee Press, 1982.

_____. *Uneven Ground: Appalachia since 1945.* Lexington: University Press of Kentucky, 2008.

Gaventa, John. *Power and Powerlessness: Quiescence and Rebellion in an Appalachian Valley.* Springfield: University of Illinois Press, 1982.

Harkins, Anthony. *Hillbilly: A Cultural History of an American Icon.* Oxford: Oxford University Press, 2008.

Hubbs, Nadine. *Rednecks, Queers, and Country Music.* Berkeley: University of California Press, 2014.

Hutton, Robert. *Bloody Breathitt: Politics and Violence in the Appalachian South.* Lexington: University Press of Kentucky, 2013.

Inscoe, John, ed. *Appalachians and Race: The Mountain South from Slavery to Segregation.* Lexington: University Press of Kentucky, 2005.

Kelley, Robin D.G. *Hammer and Hoe: Alabama Communists During the Great Depression.* Chapel Hill: University of North Carolina Press, 1990.

Kiffmeyer, Tom. *Reformers to Radicals: The Appalachian Volunteers and the War on Poverty.* Lexington: University Press of Kentucky, 2008.

Lears, T.J. Jackson. *No Place of Grace: Antimodernism and the Transformation of American Culture, 1880-1920.* Chicago: University of Chicago Press, 1981.

Lewis, Ronald L. *Black Coal Miners in America: Race, Class, and Community Conflict, 1780-1980.* Lexington: University Press of Kentucky, 1987.

_____. *Transforming the Appalachian Countryside: Railroads, Deforestation, and Social Change in West Virginia, 1880-1920.* Chapel Hill: University of North Carolina Press, 1998.

McDonald, Michael J. and John Muldowny. *The TVA and the Dispossessed: The Resettlement of Population in the Norris Dam Area.* Knoxville: University of Tennessee Press, 1981.

Portelli, Alessandro. *They Say in Harlan County: An Oral History.* Oxford: Oxford University Press, 2010.

Pudup, Mary Beth, Dwight B. Billings, and Altina Waller, eds. *Appalachia in the Making: The Mountain South in the Nineteenth Century.* Chapel Hill: University of North Carolina Press, 1995.

Purcell, Aaron. *White Collar Radicals: The TVA's Knoxville Fifteen, the New Deal, and the McCarthy Era.* Knoxville: University of Tennessee Press, 2009.

Rice, Connie Park and Marie Tedesco, eds. *Women of the Mountain South: Identity, Work, and Activism.* Athens: University of Ohio Press, 2015.

Satterwhite, Emily. *Dear Appalachia: Readers, Identity, and Popular Fiction Since 1878.* Lexington: University Press of Kentucky, 2011.

Scott, Rebecca. *Removing Mountains: Extracting Nature and Identity in the Appalachia Coalfields*. Minnesota: University of Minnesota Press, 2010.

Shapiro, Henry D. *Appalachia on Our Mind: The Southern Mountains and Mountaineers in the American Consciousness, 1870-1920*. Chapel Hill: University of North Carolina Press, 1978.

Shiflett, Crandall. *Coal Towns*. Knoxville: University of Tennessee Press, 1995.

Straw, Richard and H. Tyler Blethen. *High Mountains Rising: Appalachia in Time and Place*. Springfield: University of Illinois Press, 2004.

Turner, William H., Edward J. Cabbel and Nell Irvin Painter, eds. *Blacks in Appalachia*. Lexington, University Press of Kentucky, 1985.

Thomas, Jerry Bruce. *An Appalachian New Deal: West Virginia in the Great Depression*. Morgantown: West Virginia University Press, 2010.

Waller, Altina L. *Feud: Hatfields, McCoys, and Social Change in Appalachia, 1860-1900*. Chapel Hill: University of North Carolina Press, 1988.

Williams, John Alexander. *Appalachia: A History*. Chapel Hill: University of North Carolina Press, 2002.

FILMS & VISUAL ART

Before the Mountain Was Moved, dir. Robert K. Sharpe, 1970.

Blood on the Mountain, dir. Mari-Lynn Evans and Jordan Freeman, 2016.

Burke, Bill. *Portraits*, 1987.

Chemical Valley, dir. Mimi Pickering and Anne Lewis Johnson, 1991.

Dotter, Earl. *The Quiet Sickness: A Photographic Chronicle of Hazardous Work in America*.

Gowin, Emmet. *Photographs*, 1976.

Goodbye Gauley Mountain: An Ecosexual Love Story, dir. Beth Stevens and Annie Sprinkle, 2014

Harlan County, U.S.A., dir. Barbara Kopple, 1978.

Kentucky Route Zero, videogame designed by Jake Elliott and Tamas Kemenczy for Cardboard Computer.

The Last Mountain, dir. Bill Haney, 2011.

May, Roger. *Testify: A Visual Love Letter to Appalachia*. Durham: Horse and Buggy Press, 2014.

Night in the Woods, videogame designed by Alec Holowka, Scott Benson, and Bethany Hockenberry for Infinite Fall and Finji.

Queer Appalachia Collective. *Electric Dirt*, 2017.

Rothstein's Last Assignment, dir. Richard Knox Robinson, 2011.

Sludge, dir. Robert Sayler, 2005.

Spear, David M. *The Neugents: Close to Home*, 2010.

Stranger with a Camera, dir. Elizabeth Barret, 1999.

Up the Ridge, dir. Nick Szuberla and Amelia Kirby, 1999.

PEOPLE, PROGRAMS, AND ORGANIZATIONS (THANK YOU)

100 Days in Appalachia, Appalachian Group to Save the Land and People, Appalachian Queer Film Festival, Appalachian Feminist Coalition, Appalachian Land Study I & II, Appalachian Volunteers, Appalshop, Black Appalachian Commission, Beehive Collective, Black Lung Association, Judy Bonds, Anne and Carl Braden, Jackie Bernard, Brookside Women's Club, Calls from Home, Camp Happy Apalachee, Catholic Committee of Appalachia, Center for Coalfield Justice, Center for Rural Strategies, Coal Employment Project, Coal River Mountain Watch, Widow Combs, Communication Workers of America, Bruce Crawford, Hazel Dickens, Rick Diehl, Muriel Dressler, Wilma Dykeman, Zylphia and Myles Horton, Freyda Epstein, Friends of Blair Mountain, Friends for Environmental Justice, Jim Garland, Larry Gibson, Father Joe Hacala, Granny Hagar, Sarah Ogan Gunning, Sid Hatfield, Highlander Research and Education Center, Inside Appalachia, Kentuckians for the Commonwealth, John Kobak, Aunt Molly Jackson, Mother Jones, Letcher County Governance Project, Helen Lewis, John L. Lewis, Hawk Littlejohn, Miners for Democracy, Mountain Association for Community Economic Development, Mud Creek Health Clinic, North Carolina Harm Reduction Coalition, Radical Action for Mountains' and People's Survival, Florence and Sam Reece, Ola Belle Reed, Redneck Revolt, Stay Together Appalachia Youth, Lee Smith, John and Katherine Tiller, Trillbillies, United Mine Workers of America, Don West, Ella Mae Wiggins, Young Appalachian Leaders and Learners.

ACKNOWLEDGEMENTS

I would like to thank a number of friends and colleagues whose support has shaped this book as much as their words and deeds. I am grateful to Anne Trubek and Martha Bayne for seeing the potential for this book in a handful of online essays I wrote about Appalachia and the 2016 election. Their mentorship and guidance made the creation of this book feel like a family affair. Thank you to David Wilson, who drew the exceptional cover of this book, to Meredith Pangrace, Belt Publishing's graphic designer, and to Michael Jauchen, our style editor. I am especially appreciative of Aaron Bady for reading and commenting on drafts, and for passing along early critical suggestions that improved the text greatly. Thank you to Michelle Blankenship, who handled publicity for this book. To all those at Belt Publishing who helped bring this book into being, thank you.

I am grateful for the friendship of John Edwin Mason and Roger May. Our conversations about Appalachia and photography inspired me to write and think more deeply about our region. To Crystal Good, thank you for the inspiration of your poetry and your entrepreneurial spirit. Thank you also to Lou Murrey for your commitment to the region, including my home turf, East Tennessee, and for the gift of your gorgeous photography. I am indebted to Chris Offutt, who generously offered fiction, poetry, and photography recommendations that have improved the back matter and who gave my work an important boost. Thank you to Tressie McMillan Cottom for reading and commenting on this book, and most of all, thank you for proving to me that you're never too old to find new intellectual role models. A warm thank you to my Whitesburg friends Tayna Turner, Tom Sexton, and Tarence Ray for not only talking the talk with your fantastic podcast, but also walking the walk in your activism. To Glenn Taylor, who offered to give a copy of my book to Huey Perry, a personal hero—you made my day.

There are a number of historians and scholars of Appalachia whose work has been invaluable to me. Dwight Billings, Kathleen Blee, Wilma Dunaway, Ronald Eller, John Gaventa, Anthony Harkins, Bob Hutton, John Inscoe, Tom Kiffmeyer, Ron Lewis, Alessandro Portelli, Rebecca Scott, Henry Shapiro, William Turner, John Alexander Williams, and others mentioned in the back matter, thank you for making the road by walking.

I am especially thankful for my partner, Josh Howard. He did something far more important than offering scholarly suggestions and support during the writing of this book—he took me home. Josh didn't hesitate when I proposed living and working in Appalachia again, and he made a tremendous professional sacrifice to bring us closer to the people and places that matter the most to us. On that note, I am also grateful to our families for giving us a warm welcome when we returned.

This book is dedicated to the memory of my grandfather, G.C. Monroe, who passed away just before we went to press. My grandfather was the warmest, most gentle man I have ever known. He was raised on a mountain in Virginia and it is fitting that we have found our new happiness here in a place that reminds me so much of him. When I think of my grandfather, I hear Walt Whitman in my head: "For every atom belonging to me as good as belongs to you." I am grateful for the gift of his memory, and the memories of men and women like him, who raised us and radicalized us with tremendous kindness, love, and solidarity.

ABOUT THE AUTHOR

Elizabeth Catte is a writer and historian from East Tennessee. She holds a PhD in public history from Middle Tennessee State University and is the co-owner of Passel, a historical consulting and development company.